CATCH
YOUR BREATH...

It's a New

Beginning

**A 40 day journey towards
a new year, a new season or a new start**

K.L. KANDEL

ISBN-13: 978-0615943084

Unless otherwise identified, all Scripture quotations
in this publication are taken from the Holy Bible:
New International Version. (2011). Grand Rapids,
Mich.: Zondervan. Used by permission; and the
King James Version (KJV).

About K.L. Kandel

K.L. Kandel is the pen name for Kris Kandel Schwambach, Karen Kandel Kizlin, Kathie Kandel Poe and Linda Kandel Mason, four sisters with some very different life experiences.

As mothers, grandmothers, teachers, and Bible teachers, their writing reveals a sense of wonder, discovery and a heart to connect with the hearts and homes of those around them.

Learn more, explore additional writings, and contact K.L. Kandel at **www.klkandel.com**.

Also By K.L. Kandel

Take A Deep Breath...

It's Christmas

---

*A 40 Day Journey
Towards The Heart Of Christmas*

Learn more at **www.klkandel.com**.

Special Thanks

When the phone rang and the young man's voice on the other end asked to speak to my husband, I did not realize that it was a life changing moment. My husband came downstairs after the call and said that Jeremy Secrest wanted permission to date our middle daughter. In that very moment I knew. He would become our son, the perfect spouse for our daughter Joy. But Jeremy is not just my son-in-law; he is the creative genius behind our books. We give him the text and he makes it beautiful.

The cover, the design, the layout, are all from your creative soul. How do we ever say thanks for all that you do, Jeremy? You are an author in your own right. (Jeremy's book is called *Creative You*, available on Amazon.) Yet, you take the time to work on ours. We are blessed. Thank you!

Cinnamon rolls are on the way.

Love,

Aunt Linda, Aunt Kris, Aunt Kathie, and Mom

Dedication

Marriage, the birth of children, graduations, the birth of grandchildren, joys, but also sometimes sorrows...these are life altering events that cause us to catch our breath. We know we are standing at the entrance to a new beginning.

We want to say thank you to our family and friends who live these moments with us. We love you all. You are a part of the story.

We want to dedicate this book to our Lord and Savior Jesus Christ. We love You. You ARE the Story.

Table Of Contents

Preface

Do you have your cup of coffee? Why don't you go and get it? We'll wait.

It has been a busy time hasn't it? Shopping, lights, parties, worship experiences, joy and laughter and twinkling eyes, maybe some of the trees have been sugar coated with snow. It has all been wrapped up in one beautiful season.

And now it's time to catch our breath and start with a new page, a new beginning.

We are asking you to walk with us for a few minutes to laugh, get a little serious and maybe even be challenged from time to time.

But we only want you to take a few moments in the pages of our book. What we hope is that we will all be escorted into the pages of His Book...a few moments with us, many moments with Him.

There is such an adventure in His Word and we can begin there today. So grab your coffee. (Our brothers say it is Biblical based on *"Hebrews"* and keeping us *"grounded"*. Do you see why we haven't asked for their help to write this book? More about them later!)

Are you ready? Okay.

Catch your breath... It's a new beginning.

Introduction

"Tradition...Tradition!" In the musical, *Fiddler on the Roof*, Tevye sings about tradition and dances to it because tradition is so very important to his family. Traditions are important. We have just come through the Christmas season with a lot of our traditions, customs and special familiar moments. Traditions are carved into us from some of our earliest memories. They dictate the food at Christmas, involvement in Christmas pageants, songs that are sung, the time of the gift giving and even specific locations where presents are opened. But there are January traditions as well. People eat certain foods as they ring in the beginning of a new year. Some families eat herring. There are places where people eat one grape for every chime of the clock as it strikes midnight. Some eat black-eyed peas, and others eat pomegranates.

Now, we don't know where this began, but our family's tradition is sauerkraut, cooked all day on a bed of pork so that the smell wafts and permeates into every nook and cranny of the house. To put it mildly, the house reeks. Sauerkraut is one of those foods, that when cooking, it draws flies. Flies like what is dead and rotting. If you cook it in the summer they line up at the screen door with a fork in one hand and a knife in the other, because sauerkraut is dead, fermented cabbage. Even before it dies and is fermented, cabbage actually has its own certain foulness. So kill it, let it rot for a season, and presto, you have the makings of a fabulous holiday meal.

That is of course, unless you marry into the family. If you haven't grown up with this, your nose has not developed the capacity to appreciate the finer nuances of the aroma hidden in the roasting kraut. And my son-in-law did not grow up with this tradition. So when he was invited to Grandma's house for New Year's Day, he did not realize it was the smell of dinner. He thought it was the pungent, musty odor of old. Old socks? Old shoes? What in the house could smell like that? He had to walk outside to catch his breath. But the next year New Year's was at his house and his wife was cooking dinner. When he walked in and smelled that same aroma, he again caught his breath and must have had to ask himself, *"How many sunrises and sunsets have I lived through to get this old?"*

The smell of old, it's nice when it's a piece of old weathered furniture, or an ages old book. Old is good when it comes to our beloved parents and grandparents, and great grandparents, their wisdom and counsel and love, a much cherished commodity. But old habits, old hurts, old hang-ups, old stinky socks, perhaps it's time to let go of those and begin fresh.

So just as the New Year often begins with tradition, it also holds a challenge...begin something new. Resolutions, changes, commitments, fresh starts, all can begin.

Day 1

At a little country church in Robertsville, Ohio, a Sunday school teacher issued a challenge to a group of fifth graders, *"Read your Bible every day for a week."*

It was a message of only a few words. It wasn't the deep, profound, scholarly, theological, teaching that one would expect to be life changing. This was eight words, a simple challenge tossed out to a bunch of kids.

Now let me interrupt my story with a commercial. Along with the idea of new beginnings, if you are looking to begin serving and you don't know exactly where you will fit, why not try children's ministry? If you want to lead people to Christ, work with kids. Their minds are open, their hearts receptive. More people come to Christ as children than they do as adults. Even in the nursery, rocking little people to sleep is a tremendous moment to pray for that child, that family, that home. Prayer, teaching, a few words thrown out to children, who knows the impact!

Okay, commercial is over, those eight words changed the lives of three little girls. We read our Bibles that week and the next and the next until that challenge began a lifelong habit of reading God's Word every single day.

ONE TEACHER, EIGHT WORDS, AND THREE
CHANGED LIVES.

Sadly, we never told our Sunday School teacher the
impact she had. By the time we were old enough to
realize that she might have liked to know, she had
already gone to heaven. I do know this, someday
in heaven I will find Pauline Rue, wrap my arms
around her and say, *"Thank you, you made a huge
difference."*

But reading the Bible was just the beginning, because just reading the Bible, is not loving the Bible.
I did it. I read the Bible every day, but it felt a little
like swallowing a spoonful of medicine. It didn't
have to taste good. I knew it would help me get
better. Studying the Scripture was much more duty
than delight. Please understand, our great God used
even that minimal effort on my part to teach me
and draw me near to His heart. But I have discovered that there is so much more.

The difference came in the early nineties, not my
nineties, the 1990's. I knew that others had a closer
relationship with the Lord and I wanted that too, so
I began to pray a very simple prayer. *"Lord, send a
revival, but please let it begin with me."*

I felt a little like Jacob in Genesis 32:22-32. Feel
free to open your Bible and read this account. Jacob
told the Lord he would not let go until the Lord

blessed him. Don't let go, hold on, ask God to bless.

And you know what? God answered. I thought He would, no surprise there, He just didn't do it the way I expected. Hmmm, seems like there's a message in that.

I thought there would be some awesome church service when God would challenge my heart and I would be changed. Yep! God could have done that. He changed people in the Bible. But that was not how He worked with me. Instead, He began to lift the veil on His Word and it became a Book I could not put down. Before, I had just read it, but I began to experience it. Jesus was waiting in the shadow of every page, living, breathing His message to my heart. Studying the Bible has become an adventure. I discovered a secret: there's treasure in the Book. I discovered another secret: our lives are transformed when we spend time in His Word.

Okay, new beginnings...new starts...new challenges... Here's ours: Read your Bible every day for a week. But don't just read it, meet Him.

During these winter days with the holidays over, and the pace slowing down, it is, indeed, time to catch our breath. You might want to grab a pen along with your coffee or hot chocolate. You just might want to write something in your Bible that He says to you, that He whispers to your heart.

Those are life-changing, heart stopping moments when you know that the God of the universe has spoken to you.

Today, right now, we can breathe in His sweetness, His presence, His very essence. What will He teach us? How will He speak? What treasure will we find along the way? Perhaps we will ascend to great heights as we climb mountains to see His face. Perhaps we will descend to new depths never traveled before as we go deep into His Word. I am fully convinced that we can never exhaust His Book, but we can daily take flight on its wings or plumb its depth. Can you tell I'm excited to see what new moments await?

So we begin.

Genesis 1

If this is a new beginning, then the logical place
to begin is at the beginning, the book of Genesis.
The name means beginning. It is the first book in
the Bible. Now, we aren't going to hurry through.
There are great Bible reading programs where you
read through the Bible in a year. This isn't that.
The Bible is a big book, not just in its length but
in its depth. God authored it, so would we expect
anything less? We are going to stop and linger, and
smell the sweetness, taste it, savor each passage.
We won't get it all. That, my friends, is impossible.
But let's look for the truth, hidden behind the truth,
to see The Truth.

Genesis 1:1 begins, *"In the beginning..."* The book of
Genesis tells us the beginning of just about everything
except God, because God has always been. We learn
about the birth of our world, creation, the beginning of man, the creation of a woman, marriage,
evil, the birth of sin, the consequences of sin, the
birth of a first child, the death of a second, sadness,
toil, the birth of rebellion, the birth of languages,
the birth of a nation, and on and on. But more
importantly, the book of Genesis holds the promise
of the birth of a Savior for a sinful, fallen world.

Wow! One book and it contains all that, with so
much more. Then the first verse continues, *"In the
beginning God..."* This Book is about God. He was

there in the beginning. He is here now and He will continue to be here with every new beginning, every final goodbye, and every moment in between.

Now I want us to remember that the Bible isn't just about reading. It is also about applying His Word to my life. Here is the question. Is there an application in these first four words for us? For me this verse is an invitation to begin my day with Him. *"In the beginning God..."* Start out with a few moments, or a few more than a few, pray, study, give the day to Him.

Oh, and don't forget you might want your coffee. Coffee with Jesus at the beginning of each day, breathing in the joy of His Word...what a gift.

Today is a new beginning. It's starting to feel a little like Christmas all over again.

Day 2

Okay, so I was told that my sister was half my size. (I told this story in our first book, *Take a Deep Breath...It's Christmas*.) The lady who said it was not intending to tell me I was overweight. She was trying to say my sister was thin. But the results were the same. I felt fat. And you know what that did? It made me take a look at myself and agree.

When something makes you take a good look, it's time to do something about it. Now don't get me wrong, I didn't go on a crash diet of hummus and lettuce wraps or half a cup of yogurt a day. I didn't try to lose fifty pounds in two months. I didn't do anything extreme. (Although there is one upside to the colonoscopy that my doctor ordered...I lost a couple of pounds. It's just that the process is, well, let's just say, not that fun). I have managed, though, to cut down a little each week. The pounds have not gone off nearly as fast as they went on. I can easily pack on ten pounds in a weekend without even trying. It's amazing how fast they can get added on and how slowly they come off.

But I did start. Today I am thirty pounds less and when I go back to track it I guess I have lost about two and a half pounds a month (including the colon cleanse). Boy, that seems like so little, but the good news is that it's thirty pounds less than it was last year.

So how did I do it?

I started...I started that day. I didn't say I would start on Monday. I did not say I would start on January 1st. I didn't even tell myself I would begin tomorrow. I told myself I was going to eat a little less beginning then. I made a commitment that it would be okay to go to bed a little bit hungry. I would count what I ate (and most days I've been able to do that) and when I got to the number of calories I intended to eat for the day, I would stop. It has made me be a little more conscious about the cake staring me in the face at a birthday party. It's not that I can't eat it. I can eat it if I want; I just have to count it.

In Luke 14:28 Jesus asked if someone wanted to build a tower shouldn't he sit down and count the cost.

Well, I wasn't building a tower but as big as I was getting maybe I was close. I understand that this is not the primary meaning of this verse yet it's still a reminder that whatever we are building we need to count the cost. So I started counting. What was the cheesecake going to cost me? What about the second hamburger when actually I felt pretty full on just one? Did I really need the soda when water would actually quench my thirst and water adds no calories?

Today can be a new beginning. Just begin. Whatever it is that needs a change in your life, start today.

It is a day of new beginnings.

Genesis 1, Luke 24, Isaiah 53

Starting fresh, starting over, God knew we would need that. He built it into the very core of our lives. Every day begins just like all those thousands of days before it. The sun kisses the horizon and it bursts into its song of color, chasing away the darkness. And yet each new day is entirely different with a clean slate, and new possibilities. Each day contains the unknown, the unforeseen, the new.

And a new year feels like an even bigger new start. What will this one bring? Perhaps some of the sweetest moments we have ever experienced, perhaps some of the most difficult.

Sometimes we make up our minds to look better, or act better, or even be better. And the question is, better than who? God did not make us like we are so we can compare ourselves to someone else. He created us so we could know Him, become like Him. Jesus wants us to start our new year with a heart that surrenders to His will, from what we eat, to how we dress, our career, our spouses, our daily encounters. Our life isn't just about us, it is absolutely about Him.

So this year, my highest goal is simply to know the Lord better, to follow more closely, to not just know the Scripture, but to know the Author in all His beauty. I want to see the Lord, hear His voice, and to walk and talk with Him.

Luke 24:45 *"Then He opened their minds so they could understand the Scripture."* Let's begin our study of the Scripture by asking Him to open our minds also.

Father, the Bible is a big book and it seems at times a little intimidating and hard to understand, but it is what You gave us so we could know You. Please open my eyes to all that You want me to see in Your Word today. Please open my mind so I can understand. Open my heart to receive and my ears to hear Your voice. My heart's desire is that this year will be an adventure of walking with You, my Creator, Savior, my Lord and my Friend. Thank You. I approach Your Word with eager anticipation.

Amen

But it is really hard not to compare ourselves with others, sometimes it even gets done for us. In this life there are always going to be comparisons. There will always be somebody prettier, or someone smarter, or skinnier, or better at a sport or more accomplished at an instrument. It is a rare thing to be dubbed the most beautiful, the most handsome, the smartest, the most talented, the best in the world. And even if you are somehow named *"the best"*, that fame lasts only a moment. There is always someone waiting in the wings to take your place and we will always be the loser in that world.

So when I feel that sting of comparison, I remember that Jesus was not deemed handsome. His appearance was not the stuff of legends. Isaiah 53:2 tells us, *"He had no beauty or majesty to attract us to Him, nothing in His appearance that we should desire Him."*

It was not His face that drew the crowds; it was His heart, His compassion, His overwhelming love. I can't change the face I have, at least not without a boatload of surgery, but I can daily let Him change my heart. And His beauty is the beauty that will stay even when the bloom is off the rose. (And believe me that bloom left a long time ago). The heart can grow more beautiful. It can grow lovely in its desire to become just like Jesus. Let's enter that beauty contest.

"In the beginning God..." If we begin and end with that, there is nothing else that matters, because it is all about Him.

Day 3

I love snow. I can't help it. Oh, I know there are
those who see the first flakes and want to run
for the beach. Their thoughts of donning gloves,
scarves, boots, and wool coats to brave an icy world
almost bring despair.

But to those who see winter that way, I have to feel
a little sad.

You are missing it!

Snow shouts of expectations that we only get to
experience when the flakes fall and the winds blow.

It brings steaming cups of hot chocolate with candy
canes, sledding down a snow packed hill, schools
cancelled, businesses closed and of course a majesty
and breathtaking beauty that only comes as a
blanket of white wraps up muddy streets, browned
grass, and sleeping trees.

And if it happens to arrive at Christmas time, all the
better, because it hugs the lights strung on branches
casting an almost magical glow.

A special kind of silence settles over everything
when a winter storm dances in. As the dirt is

covered, this brand new white world whispers in hushed tones. For those who are listening carefully, it is quoting Isaiah 1:18 *"Though your sins are like scarlet, they shall be as white as snow..."*

The world is transformed into a giant object lesson of new beginnings.

You see, it brings a promise. This promise means you can start over.

I know because there was a breathtaking moment in time when I received that promise. I invited Jesus into my life and it was as if every sin I had ever thought, spoken, or done was placed under a blanket of snow and washed clean. I was given a new beginning.

I love snow. I can't help it.

For me it speaks the promise that I get to start again.

Genesis 1

Not one of us was there. In fact not a single human witnessed the event, no eyewitnesses, except God. He gives us the account. He tells us what happened. This is what the Scripture says, *"In the beginning God created..."* Genesis 1:1.

God tells us that He created all that we see, hear, taste and know. He created it, and since He never lies, and since He is completely trustworthy, I believe.

Now that may seem to some naive, or non-intellectual, but I find it completely in keeping with what is in the world around me. We live in a magnificent world. The beauty is breath taking, the views so stunning at times that we are moved to tears.

Our world is intricate and created so incredibly that it couldn't be random. It screams design. The tilt of the earth, our distance from the sun, the exact correct speed with which our world rotates is not an accident.

The heavens declare God's glory, the stars sing, there is order, there is law, we have truth that we stand on, all from the hand of God.

There are plants that need specific insects in order for pollination to occur. There are insects that can't exist without specific plants. Even one-celled organisms are incredibly complex.

And then there are humans. Our bodies, our brains, the human eye, the irreducible complexity is mind-boggling. Do you see the evidence of God's beautiful design?

And there is so much more.

Genesis 1:1 *"In the beginning God created..."*

Day 4

I hate ice. Ice is icy. (Now isn't that a creative way to say that?) But it's true.

Oh, it can be beautiful when it swallows up an evergreen branch or clutches its fingers on a leaf-bare tree. But ice can also have a death grip on the world. It can turn out the lights and turn off the heat.

I know. I lived it.

My son and daughter-in-law had just given birth to their second little boy. He was one week old when they moved here. Our son was taking a new job and they didn't have their own home yet. We were delighted that they moved in with us.

But I am not a bit sure that they would use the word *"delight"*. They had no idea what they were walking into.

Have you ever heard an ice storm move in? It sounds like broken glass. We heard it that night as we went to bed. I knew when my head hit the pillow that school would be cancelled and I love snow days!

But I didn't know...no, I just didn't know. (Can you hear my voice trailing off?) And then the fun began.

Sometime in the middle of the night my daughter's family showed up because the heat was out in their house. They let us know of their dilemma by tossing chunks of ice onto our second story window. (They didn't want to wake the new baby.)

We got them settled and then the grandparents, in-laws, nieces, nephews, friends started appearing. They didn't come out of the woodwork. They came out of the ice chest.

This iced-in event went on for a week. I fed, did laundry, made beds for at least thirty different people that week. We had heat and electricity while most of the city did not. Some stayed long enough to get warm and some moved in. It felt a little like the grandparent's bed in the Willy Wonka story. It was scary funny. Eighty year olds wrapped in fleece robes and all of the kids wanting chocolate, but believe me, there was no golden ticket.

I am not blessed with the gift of hospitality. I am not a good cook. I have been known to throw a cleaning rag in with a bunch of laundry and have everything come out smelling like furniture polish. A week socked in with me probably served as an unwanted diet and left our guests needing to shop for new underwear.

And so it was that I found myself flung over a shopping cart weeping about which kind of cereal to buy. It was overwhelming. It wasn't that I didn't want to help, I just couldn't quite figure out how to get it all together.

And then the fireworks began!

My son asked me to step outside to talk with me. It was dark. It was cold. Outside was the last place I wanted to be. If he had called me out to complain that their two little boys and his sweet, brave wife were getting cabin fever, I would have certainly understood. But that is not what he wanted to discuss.

All he said was, *"Mom, look!"*

He pointed to a large tree next to our home. It was ice covered with hanging branches. And apparently one of those branches wanted to warm up so it kept kissing the power lines. With every smack of its lips, sparks flew... EVERYWHERE!

He wanted to warn me of how dangerous this scenario was.

It left me with a choice. We could ask the power company to cut the power. Or we could possibly watch our roof catch fire and have to call a fire drill that left us standing in the street, barefoot, shivering, huddled masses yearning to breathe free...wait a minute, that's another story. But you get my drift. (Does ice drift?)

So what did I do?

I chose the only sane option. I prayed. I walked into the house, nearly frozen, tears waiting behind my eyes and I prayed. I didn't pray on my knees until I heard the Lord say it would be alright. I didn't pray until I felt the burden of fear lift. I just prayed. After all I had cold cereal to cook and laundry to ruin. So I just prayed.

It wasn't long. It wasn't earth shattering. But it was ice shattering. Within a very short time the branch broke and hit the ground. The crisis was over. Did you hear me? The branch broke and the crisis was over!

Little thing? Not to me. Yes, my prayer was little. My stamina was little. My faith was probably pretty little. But His answer was big. His answer told me He was watching out for me.

Ice isn't a problem for Him. The cold doesn't shut Him out. He doesn't need to be wrapped in a fleece blanket to stay warm. He doesn't care if I burn the cold cereal. He cares about me.

If I am watching, I can see it. If I am listening, I can hear Him. If I will turn away from the problems and walk straight into His arms, He will wrap me in His fleece blanket and I can hear Him whisper *"I love you!"*

Every moment of every day, I can walk into His big bear hug and let Him take care of me.

Do I still have to cook? Do I still have to do laundry, or vacuum, or shop for bargains? Yes. My daily life is just a daily life.

But it begins every morning with a whisper.
"I love you!"

If you listen, you can hear it too.

Genesis 1

Genesis 1:1-2, *"In the beginning God created the heavens and the earth. Now the earth was formless and empty, darkness was over the surface of the deep, and the Spirit of God was hovering over the waters."*

The earth was not complete, not at this point a finished work. It was formless, dark, covered in water, not the beauty that we see today. Yet, even before it was finished, even in its darkness, there was the Spirit of God hovering right above.

The Bible uses the word *"hovering."* I'm a mom. I'm a grandmother, I know hovering. Hovering is close; it's personal. Hovering protects even when the one hovered over isn't aware. Hovering is love that cares deeply. I don't want my little ones hurt. I hover because then I am right there if they need me.

The picture in this passage is that of a mother hen, gathering her chicks near to her breast and surrounding them with her wings, fluttering, so close and protective. She is keeping them warm, keeping them safe, ready to peck the daylights out of any assailant. I should know, she went after me once, another story. Again, I know hovering.

That was the nearness of God at the very birth of the world. He wasn't far from His creation. He wasn't distant. Even in its incomplete state God was right there. And then God did every bit of the work of completing our incredible planet and universe. God did it!

Do we see? God did ALL the work of completing His creation. It was not the task of the creation to finish the work. It was God's. That blesses the dirty stinky socks right off of me, because I look at my own life and see the incompleteness, the darkness. I know I am not a finished work. I know I sin and yet, even in my incomplete state, He is so near.

Philippians 1:6 says. *"...being confident of this, that He who began a good work in you will carry it on to completion until the day of Christ Jesus."*

HE will carry it on to completion.

The word for Spirit in the Hebrew is Ruah; it means breath. He's hovering over us. His spirit so close we can breathe it in. His loving arms waiting to draw us near. And God has already done every bit of the work needed to complete us, and wash away the sin of the world.

It happened on a day when the world once again was plunged into darkness and Jesus cried out, *"It is finished"*. At that very moment all the work of salvation was done. There's not a thing we need to add to it. He did it all. The magnificent beauty with which He completed the world is the magnificent beauty that He wants to pour into our very lives when we say *"Yes"*.

What a gift! I think I hear sleigh bells.

Day 5

I hate ice in an ice storm when there is no electricity.

Kris had heat, light, and a houseful of guests. My guests arrived and suddenly we heard a POP! POP! Then the lights and heat and stove went out.

Now let me set the record straight. I do know that there have been whole people groups throughout history who have lived quite successfully in the icy reaches of the world. They build homes out of ice, walk on carpets of ice and sleep on beds carved into the ice. They do, however, have seal skin rugs and polar bear blankets to stave off the icy cold and they, of course, have blubber.

Why? Well...because...it's...first of all... DELICIOUS! Seriously, I saw someone on TV say this. You know... fried blubber, blubber baked into a casserole or even roasted with a soupcon (that's a French culinary word meaning a hint or just a little) of blubber seasoning. And of course the ever favorite, blubber pops in the icy cold tundra.

But also because blubber is abundant. When you hook a six ton whale on your fishing line you have a lot of blubber and really, who ever throws out perfectly good blubber?

But most importantly blubber adds a thin or perhaps thick layer of cold-warding-off fat to the body, thus keeping you warm against the cold, cold winter. And who wouldn't want that?

So, since I had neither seal skin rugs nor polar bear blankets, it was cold. The organic food store didn't carry blubber and since I had neglected to order in a case, we were ill equipped and very cold.

We were simply a huddled mass yearning to breathe free, oh wait, that's Kris' story.

We were freezing. Even in the winter sunshine the house was cold. We tried to make do with eggs fried over the fire in an iron skillet, canned soup heated in an iron kettle in the fireplace and pancakes cooked over a blazing can of sterno. But hey, it was not blubber, so the food did little to keep us warm.

But if we thought the day was cold, when the sun said goodbye and night settled in, the very icy darkness and coldness made its way in too. January without light is just plain dark. January without the light's warmth is just plain cold. So the only thing to do was curl up on our icy (not seal leather) couch, huddle under our (not polar bear) blankets, pray and fall asleep with visions of blubber plums dancing around in our heads.

My counsel to Kris? Get over it. YOU HAD HEAT!

Recipes for cooked blubber:

First catch the whale; then call me.

Genesis 1

We have already said that in the beginning there was God.

He created the heavens and the earth, but darkness covered the surface of the deep.

God hovered near and then His voice broke the silence.

"And God said, 'Let there be light,' and there was light." Genesis 1:3 The very first recorded words that echoed across our universe from the mouth of God were about glorious light, beautiful, magnificent light. And that light was good.

One of the things I love most during the Christmas season is all the light, the homes that glow with bright white lights, and the houses decorated with the gorgeous colored lights. Some twinkle and race, some spell out holiday greetings. Even under a blanket of cold snow, the light shines through. It's just lovely. The December darkness is broken up by all the light and we feel its warmth even in the bitter winter wind. December reminds us that the light is good.

One of the things I miss most in January is all the light. As the lights come down the darkness seems darker. But it isn't just in December that we can remember that the light is good. We experience the goodness of light every single day of every single month. Daily we are greeted with the breathtaking moment when the sun peeks its head over the horizon. The color is exquisite, a gift for those of us who are awake at that hour. Even on the coldest of days, the warmth and light of the sun can be seen and felt as it streams in our windows. Then there is that moment of divine perfection when the sun bids the day goodbye, and the pink, blue, orange, yellow sky reminds us that the light is such a good gift. Then too, even in the darkness of January, the night sky is illuminated with a million twinkling stars.

Every day of every month of every year, we are reminded that God's word is true. *"And God said, 'Let there be light,' and there was light. God saw that the light was good, and He separated the light from the darkness."* Genesis 1:3-4

Day 6

Yes, January is dark. It gets dark early and stays dark late. The skies are often tinged with gray looming clouds. Some days the sun barely shines. The month of January is dark. So what can we do to brighten our world?

God spoke to Linda's heart and gave her a solution. She mails a box of yellow to an unsuspecting friend.

Never heard of a box of yellow? It's a surprise of sunshine in a gift. Yellow flowers, yellow crayons, yellow candies, yellow candles, yellow tissues, one never knows when there could be a winter cold and what better way to fight it than with sunshine. She sends yellow paper plates, forks, knives and spoons, and bright yellow napkins, for a supper table filled with light. Linda packs up yellow into a present that brightens someone's day. Not only does the recipient feel better, it adds light and brightness to Linda's life to send this de-light-ful surprise.

Perhaps in the January darkness a box of yellow is just what someone might need. Spread a little sunshine.

Genesis 1, John 1

God spoke and light came.
God spoke and the sky appeared.
God spoke and the waters became seas.
God spoke and the land produced vegetation.
God spoke the lights of the heavens into existence.
God spoke the living creatures of the sea and the
living creatures of the land and there they were.

All that we see, all that is this planet we call earth,
and all that the heavens reveal is His spoken Word.
It became light and sky and trees and planets and
stars and amazing animals and beauty and majesty
and color and fruit and the quietness of snow and the
gentleness of summer breezes and the power of the
hurricane and intricate cells and on and on. He has
revealed His eternal power and His divine nature.

And He did it for us.

He did it so we could know Him, so we could
experience His great love. All of nature reveals
Him, because it came from His very heart and was
spoken from His very mouth. The spoken Word of
God became all of nature.

But He didn't stop there.

The loving God, who created, has given us His
intricate, amazing, powerful, beautiful written
Word. He has revealed His eternal power and
divine nature to us through His written Word.

He did it so we could know Him, so we could experience His great love.

And He didn't stop there.

"The Word became flesh and made His dwelling among us. We have seen His glory, the glory of the one and only Son who came from the Father, full of grace and truth." John 1:14.

Jesus has revealed God's divine nature and eternal power to us so that we could know Him, and experience His great love.

He is the Spoken Word.
He is the Written Word.
He is the Living Word.
He is love revealed.
We have His Word on it.

So when God speaks to your heart, listen. He might just be using it to bring sunshine into someone's life.

Day 7

There are patterns in our lives, routines, if you will. They help us stay on track and make sure we know where our keys are in the morning and that the kids have their backpacks ready at the door. They are good for us and help us to stay organized. Even children should have some of these, for it builds responsibility.

But sometimes we forget.

My granddaughter Faithie was only four, just a tiny girl. Every day it was her job to make sure she had her lunch with her in the car as she went to her preschool/daycare. Her lunches were very special because each one had a hand written love note from her mother with silly things like *"I love you more than pickles"* or *"I love you more than ice cream"*. They were written in different colors and had pictures drawn on them. It was her Mommy's way of saying *"I'm with you and I love you so much."* It had become the highlight of her little four-year-old world since she was at school and far away from her mother during the day.

But this day, Faithie forgot.

Her Daddy was taking her to school and she hurried to get into the car. She was excited because this was her last day of school for a whole week. They were going to Disney World the next day. So we can understand why she forgot her lunch. Daddy called Mommy and explained. But not to worry, he could just run to the grocery store on his lunch hour and get a ready-made lunch. Daddy hung up the phone.

But the more he considered it, the more he knew that would not be good enough. She needed that special love note from her mommy, so on his lunch hour he ran back home. It was almost fifteen miles each way. It took a great deal of time. Yet he loved his girl and wanted her to know it.

Lunchtime came. The children, all the little four year olds, lined up with their lunch boxes, all of them except for one. Faithie looked out the door. Daddy had said he would bring her lunch. He had told her not to worry...but he wasn't there. She looked at the other children lined up holding their own lunches and she worried. *"What if Daddy doesn't come?"* She fought back the tears, and with little shoulders slumped, walked to the cafeteria. She followed the students slowly. There was no need to hurry, when she had no lunch. Last in line she walked through the door and looked around. He was not in the cafeteria either.

No, there would be no lunch today for her. (Now in reality the day care teachers would NOT have let that happen, but she didn't know it.)

Just then a voice came. She turned around as her daddy knelt behind her and said, *"Hi Honey, I brought your lunch."*

She smiled the lovely smile of recognition, but then from sheer relief she burst into tears and threw her arms around her daddy. He had come, he had made it right on time and brought with him her own special lunch, the one with the love note that today said *"I love you more than Disney World"* written in different colors.

So do you ever feel like a four year old? I do. I look for my Father to show up and I worry. Maybe I've had a car accident, or wind damage in my yard, or a relationship that has been broken, or flooding in my basement. Maybe the checkbook doesn't have quite enough money in it so I look around wondering if He is going to show up. And, yes, I worry. But He comes and as I look back over my yesterdays, He is always right on time.

He also brings me a love note. It's written in color as well. It's red, blood red, and the note says *"I love you more than anything."*

Genesis 1

In Genesis 1, there is a pattern to each day of the creation story. It begins, *"And God said"* and then ends with, *"and there was evening and there was morning--the first day"* or *"the second day"*, etc. The pattern shows the absolute power of God. He simply spoke and it was.

His Word was enough to create.

His voice was enough to command.

This is absolutely amazing power. From darkness to light, from formless and empty to filled and teeming with life.

And we see that same power at work in and through Jesus. He rebuked the wind and the raging waters of a storm and they subsided. Instantly, there was calm. He commanded and Lazarus came out of the grave. Jesus spoke and a little girl's spirit returned. And it's what He can do in our lives. He can take empty and make it full. He can take the darkness and fill our lives with light. This God who created the world can make a new creation out of us. He can and He does every time someone receives His gift of salvation.

Day 8

The day arrived, a lovely Saturday afternoon. The planning was done. The church was decorated. The food prepared. The girls were getting ready at the church and my daughter was beautifully arrayed in her wedding gown. It was all going smoothly. All that was left for me was to run to my sister's house, she lives about thirty seconds away from the church, dress and be ready to walk in, light a candle and then enjoy the day. I donned my champagne colored suit that coordinated perfectly with the bridesmaids. Seriously, it was all going like clockwork. My husband even arrived on time to drive me back to the church.

He dropped me at the door, but as I exited the car he spoke, *"Karen, what's on the back of your dress?"*

"What? What do you mean 'what is on the back of my dress'?" I nearly ripped my skirt trying to see.

"There's something brown all over the back."

"Brown? What are you talking about brown?"

Did you catch that the dress was champagne colored? Not brown or black, but a very light shade of beige and there smeared all over the back of my suit was brown. Brown! Something brown all over the back and I was, in just a few moments, going to walk in and saunter down to the front of the church, in front of all the guests, walk up on stage and light a candle next to the perfectly dressed mother of the groom.

What had I sat in? What could it be?

My husband swallowed hard, got a sick look on his face and spoke, *"I guess... I shouldn't have been eating chocolate chip cookies in the car."*

What? Chocolate? Chocolate...on the back of my dress? Who in their right mind would think it was chocolate. It was brown. It was in the back, use your imagination to think what people would be thinking. It wasn't as if I could wear a sign that read, *"It's ok, it's only chocolate."*

"I'm sorry." He sheepishly said.

"Sorry? Sorry! Oh no! This is not an 'I'm sorry' offense. This is a 'buy me a present' offense, and it had better be a walloping big present."

I ran to the upstairs of the church where my daughters were ready and waiting. I showed them the back of my skirt.

"Think anyone will notice?"

"Mom, what did you do?"

"Your dad was eating cookies in the car."

Enough said, they understood. Fortunately my girls have a boy-scout mentality and are always prepared. My oldest ran to her car and came in with some Shout® wipes. These little miracles took the chocolate stain out and left the skirt intact. I know why they call them Shout. I shouted for joy. I don't think anyone even noticed the stain.

I called the company later to say thank you.

I'm still waiting for the walloping big present from my husband.

Genesis 1, John 2

For the most part weddings take place on the weekends, perhaps a Friday evening, a Saturday afternoon or night, even Sundays are days for weddings. Rarely does the invitation say Tuesday. But in Israel, sometimes Tuesdays are the day of choice.

We read in John chapter 2 that Jesus performed His first miracle on the third day (Tuesday) at the wedding in Cana. There is a reason for this, and it goes all the way back to Genesis 1.

Yesterday I mentioned the pattern in this chapter: And God said...and it was good, the first day. And God said... and it was good, the second day.

However, day three is a little different. Listen to what the Scripture says in Genesis 1:9-13 *"And God said, 'Let the water under the sky be gathered to one place, and let dry ground appear.' And it was so. God called the dry ground 'land,' and the gathered waters He called 'seas.' And God saw that it was good."*

"Then God said 'Let the land produce vegetation: seed-bearing plants and trees on the land that bear fruit with seed in it, according to their various kinds.' And it was so. The land produced vegetation: plants bearing seed according to their

kinds and trees bearing fruit with seed in it according to their kinds. And God saw that it was good. And there was evening, and there was morning-the third day."

Did you notice there is a double blessing on the third day? God said twice that it was good. And that's the reason it's considered a special day.

God created the land and the seas and that was good. And then He made it fruitful by creating all the vegetation and that also was good. The third day was doubly blessed.

We too can walk in that double blessing. In Christ we become a new creation and then He wants to make us fruitful...a double blessing.

So even if today is not Tuesday on the calendar, *"Happy Tuesday!"* TWO's day...get it?

Day 9

I started reading Psalm 119.

It is an acrostic poem with each of the sections using one of the twenty-two letters of the Hebrew alphabet. It means it is 176 verses long.

Believe me, reading that many verses a day was not my normal morning devotional pattern. I would usually read a few verses and that nod to the Scripture was about it. I could say I was having Bible study and felt good to go.

I don't want you to misunderstand me. The Word of God is so powerful that studying a couple of verses can be life changing. You can never get to the end of verses like John 3:16 or John 1:1.

There is mystery in the Scripture. For example in lists of names in the genealogies, when you unwrap their meaning, they literally speak the Gospel story.

And then there are the numbers. In the late 1800's a Russian born exile discovered a numeric pattern in John 1:1. This brilliant doctor, Ivan Panin, made it his life's work to discover other numeric patterns. He wrote some 40,000 pages, coming to the conclusion that this numeric fingerprint could only have been placed in the Scripture by the breath of God. He believed so strongly in what he had found that he issued a challenge through the *New York Sun* for anyone to refute his findings. No one ever could.

So I don't want you to misunderstand, you can unpack one verse for hours or days. But that was not what I was doing. I was glancing over God-breathed Words as if they were yesterday's news.

But I knew there had to be more.

One Sunday the challenge went out from our pastor to read Psalm 119 every day for a week and it would change your life.

There are a lot of things that claim they will change your life. From shampoo to tooth paste, dentures to non-stick cookware, there are claims of life transforming powers. I don't believe any of them.

But the Scripture had possibilities and I wanted a life change. So I picked up the gauntlet with a prayer, *"Lord, I'm going to read Psalm 119 every day for a week. Please let it speak to me."*

I am going to be completely transparent on this. To me, it was dry, kind of like stale bread. I just was not getting it. Wading through 176 verses every day was going to be a challenge, like swallowing old toast.

But I had started out on this journey and I was going to finish it. I wish I could tell you that at the end of seven days, my life was supernaturally transformed. After all there is something about the number seven!

But Sunday came and went and, well, nothing!

So I determined not to let go of this. I would keep on reading Psalm 119 until something happened. I had no idea what that would be.

Sunday, Monday, Tuesday, Wednesday, each day was just about the same.

I was getting ready for church that Wednesday evening when my husband came running into the house. He told me that our son had been hurt helping to put up volleyball poles for a middle school event. The nearly 100 pound base had fallen onto his foot and Dave was pretty sure Josh was going to need stitches.

My daughter and I jumped in the car and we all headed for the emergency room.

Josh did not need stitches. The emergency room doctor took one look and told us to get to Louisville as quickly as we could to the best limb specialists in the area. The hope was that they would not have to amputate some of his toes.

But they did.

It isn't necessary to give you details about the surgery. But it is my joy to give you details about the Lord's grace.

The next morning I sat at the foot of Josh's bed. I wondered how I could explain to our soccer playing son that the doctors were saying that it would be two years before he could gain back his balance and ability on the field. As he slept, I decided in the quiet to once again open my Bible to Psalm 119.

I am hard headed, can be hard-hearted, it seems, because God needed a two-by-four to get my attention.

But He got it.

I began to read and suddenly the words were jumping off the page. The Scripture had come alive!

So why am I telling you this? Because I want you to know that if it is possible in my life, it is possible in yours. God's Word is living and He wants it to live in us.

He wants us to get it!

My sisters have experienced the same kind of eye-opening adventure into His Word but it didn't take anything like it took for me. I want you to understand, it doesn't have to take a surgery to open your eyes. He just wants to open them.

By the way, about three months after the surgery, Josh's soccer coach stopped me. These were his words: *"Kris, Josh just tied the school record for the shuttle run!"*

Was it life altering for Josh? No. Did the surgery leave some scars? Yes. Josh lost two toes and his foot doesn't look all that pretty. But it has never stopped him from doing anything he really wanted to do. He laughs about the fact that it's a little hard to find flip-flops that work.

But there was a promise attached to Psalm 119. And for me it was life changing.

Shampoo? No. Dentures? Probably not.

God's Word? Absolutely! Just ask Him!

Genesis 1

"God made two great lights-the greater light to govern the day and the lesser light to govern the night. He also made the stars." Genesis 1:16

The lights in the heavens are both beautiful and functional. Sometimes the moon is so big in the night sky, it looks as if we could touch it and it illuminates the darkness. At times the sun is so bright that it hurts our eyes, but we're warmed by that brightness.

Day four of creation, God made the lights. They were placed in the heavens to separate the day and night. They were placed there as signs to mark seasons and days and years. They were put in the sky to give us light on the earth. God created them to govern the day and night, the greater light to rule the day, the lesser light to rule the night. I find that to be a convincing proof that God wrote the book of Genesis. If it were only through observation, Moses would probably have said that the large harvest moon was the greater light, but God knew which was greater.

"He also made the stars." Five words, just five little words to describe the creation of the billions, count them, the billions of stars in our universe. I love that, five simple words and we know enough. God created. He made. God did it all.

And then one of those stars became the sign, and wise men followed it and found the true Light that had come into the world to give light to every man.

Day 10

I really like TV shows about sea animals. Hunting for giant squid or searching for the megalodon shark can captivate me. Because I love those kinds of shows, I always thought that going deep-sea fishing would be great. I could just imagine seeing someone battle a giant sea creature, wrestling, struggling to reel it close to the boat and then pull up an enormous swordfish or giant blue marlin. Well, I was sure it would be fabulous. And perhaps, just perhaps, I might snag a six-ton whale, and get to bring home a tub of mouth-watering blubber just to have on hand in case of an ice storm. I wasn't worried, it keeps.

And then I went.

When you go on one of these adventures the captain tells you where to stand. So that was where I was supposed to stay. The problem was, I just happened to be positioned next to a man who was chewing tobacco. Watching someone chew is certainly bad enough but this particular man decided that depositing that chewed tobacco needed to be at his discretion. So he spit it wherever and whenever his heart desired.

Then there was the sea itself. Some days on the ocean are absolutely beautiful and serene. It's a sea of azure glass and the boat makes little ripples as it effortlessly glides through the water. This was not one of those days. The sea was referred to as choppy. Choppy means big waves make the raging water green and white. The small fishing boat was rocking back and forth, back and forth, slapping the waves as we maneuvered out deeper into the foam. I was gripping the railing trying to keep my balance and attempting to steer clear of the flying brown liquid that occasionally was blown my way.

Finally we stopped and let the anchor down so people could fish. I was trying to steady myself as well as my stomach. After a little while someone caught one. Everyone cheered. But this was not a huge beautiful fish, rather just an ordinary buy-at-the-grocery store variety.

Remember that I had been positioned. My tobacco-laced station was toward the back of the boat and the back was where they took care of the catch. What that meant was that they chopped its head off and gutted it. Blood went everywhere.

Rocky boat, tobacco juice and blood...the makings for a *"perfect storm"* in my stomach. My tobacco-chewing neighbor hadn't cared where he spit. I got to the point where I didn't care all that much where I retched. If it pooled around his feet, oh well. After a few minutes slumped at the side of the boat, the remainder of the trip was spent collapsed on a bench praying we would somehow get back to land.

My green and pale white pallor along with the waves of nausea churning inside my stomach perfectly matched the choppy sea. Deep-sea fishing? I don't think so.

Today I'm grateful that I can experience the great marvels of the ocean from my stationary living room couch and, instead of a pole, a remote in my hand.

Genesis 1

On day number five, God created the sea life, the great creatures of the sea, everything with which the water teems. Gigantic majestic whales, the tiny krill, mighty sharks, giant squid and gentle guppies, animals with shells, or fins, or tails, big tearing teeth or none at all, fish and mammals and reptiles of all colors, shapes and sizes, God placed them all in the seas. Some swim near the surface of the ocean. Some swim in its very depth where light refuses to dwell. They are amazing and wonderful creatures and God put them there.

And then He created birds: some with beautiful songs, some with beautiful feathers, some that fly long and hard, some that can't fly at all. The majestic eagle and the tiny humming bird, the reddest cardinal, the bluest bluebird, the yellow canary, the green parrot, the brown ostrich, such exquisite beauty, such exquisite design, all spoken from the mouth of God.

Beauty, design, creativity, variety, color, we stand amazed, we are brought to tears, they make us laugh, we ooh and ah.

"And God said, 'Let the water teem with living creatures, and let birds fly above the earth across the expanse of the sky.' So God created the great creatures of the sea and every living and moving

thing with which the water teems, according to
their kinds, and every winged bird according
to its kind, And God saw that it was good. God
blessed them and said, 'Be fruitful and increase
in number and fill the water in the seas, and let
the birds increase on the earth.' And there was
evening, and there was morning--the fifth day."
Genesis 1:20-23

Day 11

Animals are a gift.

Growing up both sets of grandparents lived on farms. I thought it was a prerequisite to grandparenthood. One set of grandparents had chickens and a rooster that Grandma told us to steer clear of. They had gentle cows, adorable little calves and a gigantic bull that we did not need to be told to steer clear of. He was by far the biggest animal we had ever seen.

When Grandma and Grandpa sold him, I thought they must have made a ton of money. It had to have been a lot 'cause he was a lot.

The other grandparents had pigs. In case you've never been around pigs, pigs smell. But the pigs become pork and then, when you slather on a mess of sauerkraut... well what can I say. Sometimes you just need to get past the smell to get to the delicious.

I did for the most part love the animals and was thrilled that the grandparents had them. I considered it a gift.

Now I live in a suburb, houses behind, on each side, and across the street. I can walk into the city. But my backyard seems to be a haven for woodland animals and birds. I have seen quail, raccoons, opossums, foxes, ducks, wild turkey, huge woodpeckers and tiny little ones, hummingbirds, cardinals, blue jays, about a million squirrels and rabbits, and deer, sometimes five at a time. I love the animals and I'm thrilled that they walk into my yard. I consider it a gift.

However, one night we had an animal invasion that was not such a gift. A skunk made its way into the garage and was happily munching away on the trash, and since it was pouring rain outside he was not in any hurry to leave. Wild animals should be outside, not inside. That skunk was invading our personal space, and since my husband had to drive corporate execs around in his car the next day, he was not thrilled about our visitor. In fact we were downright panicked. We did not want these executives to have to get past that SMELL to get ANYWHERE.

We strategized and came up with a plan. It was not a good plan, but it was at least A PLAN.

From the house we lobbed slices of bologna onto the driveway. We were hoping that the aroma of the bologna would lure the skunk out of the warm dry garage into the cold pouring rain. We emptied the refrigerator of bologna, we did NOT empty the garage of our skunk.

Hmmm maybe if we would have used pork cooked with fermented skunk cabbage we might have had a shot. But this skunk was not leaving...no bologna.

Second strategy: We called the fire department. We had heard that if you sprayed a skunk with CO_2, it would freeze him and you could safely carry the critter outside.

We aren't really that dumb, we were just desperate and skunk scent fogs the brain.

I think this might be a good time to say, don't believe everything you're told. Don't believe everything you read on the internet and don't believe everything you hear about CO_2 and skunks.

I think this might also be a good time to say that emergency personnel are there for EMERGENCIES. As far as we were concerned, skunk in the garage equals emergency. But for some reason they didn't see it that way.

Their first response was, *"Is this a joke?"*

But we explained that we needed them to come to spray the skunk with CO_2.

After the hysterical laughter died down, they did tell us they had a resident expert. This fireman had had five young skunks in his house while his niece was baby-sitting. Her weapon of choice to ward off those invaders was a TV antenna but every time she struck, so did they. She finally got them out but the scent lingered.

It became obvious that this brave young fireman, one of America's finest, understood our dilemma. He graciously volunteered to drive into our driveway, shine his headlights into our garage to hopefully drive the skunk back to his own environment, but not drive him to overly react.

Our third strategy: pray. It should have been our first. Before the firefighter got there some kind of mysterious skunk rapture had already occurred.

Ladies and gentleman the skunk had left the building.

Genesis 1

Our world is filled with animal life, some so small we can't see them without a microscope, some so big they could crush us. Some are deadly, some are called man's best friend. Some are wild, some are tame. Some are for food and some are for work. They are different, wonderful, incredible.

You see them on farms, you see them in the woods, and for me, there are those special moments in places like Yellowstone, where you can be surrounded by the animals of the mountains like mighty buffalo and majestic elk. You can spot the illusive big-horned sheep, the impressive moose, wolves, marmots, mountain goats, black bears, grizzly bears (Kris stared a grizzly in the face. I was pretty sure I heard him say *"Lunch"*.) There are predators and prey.

The desert teems with animals that rarely need a drink but there are others who survive only when close to great bodies of water.

There are those who thrive in the rainforest and those who survive on blubber in the icy tundra.

Animals...a gift.

"And God said, 'Let the land produce living creatures according to their kinds: the livestock, the creatures that move along the ground, and the wild animals, each according to its kind.' And it was so." Genesis 1:24.

Thank You, God.

Day 12

Our dad decided to grow worms. Yes, you heard me correctly. He decided that a worm farm in our basement would be a real moneymaker.

Now before you go thinking that our dad was a little off, let me give you some background. He was a gardener. Yes, he had a day job but one of his real passions was gardening. I know the image you get in your mind when you think garden. You envision a little patch in the back yard that had a couple of tomato plants, a stalk or two of corn, a squash, maybe a few cucumbers.

Let me interrupt myself for a moment. We have two brothers. I think we told you that. One of them absolutely hates cucumbers. He says that they were the fruit that Adam and Eve ate from the tree and it is the reason that cucumber vines have to crawl on the ground.

I just thought you would want to know that.

Okay, so back to my story. When I say garden, I don't mean something you can measure in feet. We measured it in acres. You couldn't see the end of a row of corn and planting potatoes was like tackling a hiking trail. Our dad was serious!

So he decided to raise worms. It would enrich the soil he planted and he could sell them. I hate worms. There isn't much that is as despicable as those little creatures. They slink out of their cave dwellings during a healthy rain and slither under logs.

Do they enrich the soil? Yes, but do you know how? If you can figure out which end is their face you might be able to watch them devour the already dirty dirt and then make it dirtier as the dirt makes its way out of the not face end. It is disgusting.

But it isn't just because they squirm and wiggle and do that other.

I hate them because I was forced to enter a Sci-fi movie and it featured worms. I was about six, on my way home from school, when a bunch of boys thought it would be funny to throw them on me on the school bus. I didn't know it at the time but I was a living Worm-nado! I held it together until I reached the front door of my house and then the hysteria overtook me.

Please don't write and suggest therapy. I don't want to face my fears and get over this. I can live my whole life and not deal with worms that often. I walk around them on parking lots and don't pick up logs. I am good.

But it did make going to the basement a little

daunting. There was a farm of them lurking in the cellar and sometimes I had to walk past it. I breathed hard and shivered.

So what is the point? All of us have things in our past that mark us. Some of them are as little as a worm-nado but some of them are very, very big. They haven't left just bad memories. They have left giant, ugly wounds and scars.

It might be something done to you or it might be something you've done.

So what do we do with them?

We let God use them. Everything that happens to us can be used by God to tell a story and produce a victory. There is nothing He can't turn around. Why? Because He is victory. Don't let that worm thing IN your life rob you of even one more minute OF your life.

Hundreds of years before Jesus' death, Psalm 22 was written. It describes Jesus' death so accurately that it looks like it should have been written the day after the crucifixion. But it is history written in advance and is one of the most convincing proofs that the Bible is true.

This is what verses 6-8 tell us: *"But I am a worm and not a man, scorned by everyone, despised by the people. All who see me mock me; they hurl insults, shaking their heads.'He trusts in the Lord,' they say, 'let the Lord rescue him. Let Him deliver him, since He delights in Him'."*

Those words and actions were spit out at Jesus as if He were nothing more than a worm. He was beaten beyond the ability to recognize that He was a man. He was whipped so many times that one more strike would have probably resulted in death. What happens when you are beaten like that? Do you lose control of all your bodily functions? Do you suffer complete humiliation?

A crown of thorns, nails in His hands and feet, suffocation and a sword thrust in His side are a glimpse of the physical pain He endured but nothing compared to the gut wrenching, eternity splitting judgment that God placed on Him.

He was reduced to a worm so I could be lifted to victory. He took the pain so I could be set free from it.

Genesis 1

In case you haven't noticed, I really love Genesis 1. Something amazing happens to my heart when I read it. I see the bigness of God. I experience His majesty and power with just a word.

He says *"lights in the sky"*, and there were, but He doesn't tell us everything about those heavenly lights. We can't even begin to count them. There are brilliant scientists who spend their lives discovering the secrets of the universe.

God tells us *"vegetation"*, but how many trees and plants did He create, and what have even the most learned minds not yet discovered about their usefulness?

There are crawling things, like insects and creepy wiggly worms, but what purpose does each one have?

Can we ever number the amount of fish or birds?

Genesis 1 tells us enough so that we can know, but also allows us the delight of wondering, the adventure of studying and learning about His creation. God tells us that He created, but He didn't reveal all His secrets about the creation. He gave us the privilege of standing back in amazement and realizing that there is more to know.

The joy of discovery, it is a gift from Genesis 1. Why? Because He is Elohim, The Creator God, who created us with curiosity, with the ability to learn and with the capacity for great delight when we find His truth.

"And God saw that it was good." Genesis 1:25b

Day 13

So let me share a little more about worms.

There is a particular kind of worm called the Tola'at Shani. Another name is the Crimson Worm.

They have had a very unique purpose in history. They were the source of the beautiful red dye that was once used in the Temple in Jerusalem.

In nature, this little grub would make its way up a tree and attach herself to a branch. She would give birth to her young and then give up her life as she poured out a red dye to cover them. As it washed over the larva, they were permanently stained a crimson color.

At her death the young fed on the worm's body. But after three days her remains curled up into the shape of a heart, turned white and fell to the ground like snow.

Her life was laid down for theirs.

Does that stir anything in you? It does in me.

Psalm 51:7 is a prayer. The plea is ..."*wash me, and I will be whiter than snow.*"

What is washed away?

My sin.

The Bible tells us that we are all sinners. The sin story began when the first piece of fruit was plucked from the tree in rebellion to God's Word. I was born into it and I joined it when my thoughts, actions, words also rebelled against His Word.

Jesus Christ was reduced to a worm. His blood was shed, not just to cover my sins but to wash them whiter than snow.

It is a promise that I can start over. It is a promise that my sins are gone.

God said it and it is so.

Genesis 1

Day 1-And God said...light...
and there was light

Day 2-And God said...sky...
and it was so

Day 3-And God said...land and vegetation...
and it was so

Day 4-And God said...sun, moon and stars...
and it was so

Day 5-And God said...sea animals and birds...
and it was so

Day 6-And God said...land animals...
and yes, it was so, and *"Then God said, 'Let us
make mankind in our image, in our likeness, so
that they may rule over the fish in the sea and
the birds in the sky, over the livestock, and all
the wild animals, and over all the creatures that
move along the ground.' So God created mankind
in His own image, in the image of God He created
them; male and female He created them."*

What God said, happened. It took place. It was!
God's Word is true! We can trust it. We can stand
on it. We can rest in it. We can rely on it. We can
believe it. We can put our faith in it. God said and
it was so. God said and it is so. God said and it will
continue to be so, because He is THE WORD.

Day 14

Have you ever had a real dizzy spell? I have and they aren't pretty.

The floor seems to reach out and pull you into a horizontal position while at the same time everything is swirling.

For me, they come with a fury and the only place to go is down, down on the floor, down on a bed, down. Balance is completely out of reach and the world is not a pretty place to be and I am not a pretty person to see. My husband told me I aged about twenty-five years the last time I had one!

Life is like that when things really get out of balance. Sometimes it seems the only place you can go is down.

Genesis 1

Have you noticed the incredible balance of Genesis 1? Light and darkness, we need both. Water under the expanse of sky, and water above, all are necessary. There is the sea, but also the land. The vegetation is seed bearing plants and trees that bear fruit. God made the sun for daylight, but the moon to shine at night. He created sea life to swim the oceans and birds that fly in the sky, wild animals, but also livestock. There is beautiful balance and the balance is a vital part of life.

And then God created man.

"God created man in His own image, in the image of God He created him; male and female He created them." Genesis 1:27

God created both the male and the female. Again, there is balance, and the world needs both. Mankind is made in God's image; we reflect Him. Both the male characteristics and the female exemplify part of God's image. God's strength, but also His gentleness, His judgment against sin as well as His great love toward sinners, His giving us freedom of choice, and His hovering near, male and female reflect those qualities and many more. God wants us to know Him and all of what He has created teaches us about who He is.

Day 15

We're talking about beginnings. Let me tell you ours.

It all began when our beautiful mom walked into a quiet little grocery store in northeastern Ohio. She went to buy bologna, not so glamorous, but there was a glamorous man working behind the meat counter. Her heart stopped. He was gorgeous. She asked for bologna. He obliged. The good news here is that he thought she was gorgeous as well. Her purchase made, Mom went home. She lived with her parents and two sisters on a farm and so they had plenty of their own beef and chicken. The only meat they needed was bologna, and how much of that can you use? (well, think back to the skunk story) But she went back to buy more bologna.

Finally he called her for a date. She had to work. She was a nurse working evening hours, but made it abundantly clear that she would be available at another time. And so it began, the handsome prince, well okay, a meat cutter, our dad, and the fair maiden, the fairest in the land, our mom. Love, marriage and a honeymoon in Florida.

Dad came from a family of ten kids, good-sized even in that day. But he was twenty-seven when love struck so he told Mom, *"I'm afraid I'll be an old man before I have a family."* He wanted it big and he wanted it soon. On the way home from their honeymoon he saw a stork, rolled down the window and motioned for the stork to follow. Be careful what you wish for. If Dad had only known.

The trip home took several leisurely days, but Mom was sick most of the way. Home for a few weeks she began to suspect that Dad's wish was coming true, and soon she knew for sure. The stork had indeed followed them. Being a nurse she felt comfortable waiting until her third month to see the doctor. He weighed, measured and informed her that she was five months pregnant. She informed him that she was three months along. He insisted. She insisted.

He then suspected a tumor. (We don't know which of us was the tumor. I don't think it was me.) By the seventh month they decided on an X-ray. This was long before the days of ultra sounds. Mom had gone from a petite size 5, ninety pounds to weighing in at 150 and a fifty-six inch waist. That's some tumor.

So with Mom's rapidly growing middle, Dad kept telling her she was having triplets. Playing cards he would turn up a three and just smile. Triplets! Not being a prophet, remember, he was a meat cutter, he was floored when the X-ray actually showed three babies. The doctor had not heard three heartbeats. I guess we were all in sync. Triplets are pretty common now, not so common then. Three of everything, and multiples of most things. Do you know how many cloth diapers three babies can go through in twenty-four hours? Dad was getting a big family quicker than he had hoped possible.

And then there was Dan. Not quite two years later our dear brother arrived on the scene. And then, less than another two years and our sweet little Linda showed up. Mom and Dad now had five babies under the age of four. Be fruitful and multiply; they took it to heart. Another dear sweet brother, Bill, came four years later and finally Mom and Dad's quiver was full.

Our home was blissful, six wonderful children. We never fought, never disagreed; it was like something out of a fairy tale.

Oh wait, this isn't fiction. We did fight...once, or well, maybe it was twice.

Genesis 1

"There are no children alive who fight as much as you kids!" That, my friends, is a direct quote from the MOM.

And fight we did.

We pulled hair. Kris fainted when I pulled hers. Do you think that's where her dizzy spells began? Needless to say I only did that once. We kicked, bit, hit. Okay, just forget the last few lines of the story above. We tormented each other, threatened bodily harm, left one brother in a laundry basket on the neighbor's porch. In our defense, we did leave a note.

I guess Mom's account is a little more accurate.

So we had to have rules, laws from the Dad and Mom themselves. We were not supposed to kill or hurt or wound, or leave brothers on the neighbor's porch or pull hair, or call each other names, or a whole bunch of other things. Rules, laws, *"Thou shalt not!"* And if we wanted to live in harmony with our surroundings and be able to sit, we had better follow them.

There is the thought for some that the Bible is just a bunch of don'ts. Many people believe that it is filled mostly with: Don't do this. You can't do that.

Thou shalt not.

And the truth is there are some things that God tells us not to do.

But if we are good parents, we lay down rules: Don't go in the street! Don't even go near the street! Don't leave your brother on the porch.

And then we erect a fence in the back yard. We do it to protect, to keep our children safe.

And when God says *"Don't"* or *"Thou shalt not"*, He's doing it to keep us out of the street, or to protect the innocent little brother. So there are those things we're told not to do, but there are also many wonderful commandments that we are told to do. The first commandment God ever spoke to mankind is found in Genesis 1:28 *"Be fruitful and increase in number; fill the earth and subdue it."* Nothing negative about that.

Our wonderful creative God could have filled the world with people. He didn't. He gave us the joy of that task. He allowed us the sweetness of bringing children into the world and in the process He gave us a hint, a small taste of the joy and pleasure He felt when He created man.

Day 16

When the doctor told me that I have a brain tumor, it sounded a little like I might be staring death in the face and I wasn't sure who would blink first. Being given that information was a little daunting. The information we were not given was even more daunting.

We headed for Vanderbilt.

On the way we prayed about several things. We wanted peace, God's will, a doctor who would speak to us in terms we could understand, and healing.

I had the name of the doctor and his office number. My husband Dave dropped me off and went to park the car. I found the office and saw a huge sign above the door. It said *"Oncology."* I thought I was seeing a neurologist. I didn't know I was seeing a cancer specialist. As I stepped into the waiting room, I have to admit, I swallowed very hard and tears came to my eyes. I saw scarves and hats covering hairless heads and a death pallor that I recognized from my dad's battle with cancer.

What did it mean that I was filling out paperwork for this office?

I didn't have to wait long. I was called into his office before Dave had even had a chance to park the car. (We found out later that they had valet parking.)

Dave joined me within a few moments. When you sit in an office like that, you know there are several different directions that the conversation can go. It can be bad news. It can be really bad news. The news can be hopeful. Or the news can be great and you can catch your breath.

My news was great.

The tumor was not malignant. It would not require surgery unless it should grow larger. It meant an MRI from time to time and some medication. He did tell me that the MRI showed some brain damage. There are certainly some people in my life who would think that that explained a lot! (Do you remember that the doctor suspected a tumor when our mother was pregnant? Let me reiterate that I have a tumor; I am NOT the tumor. So do the math, it only leaves Kath. I'm just saying...)

Dave noticed a small cross on the collar of the doctor's lab coat. He asked him about it. He told us he was a follower of Jesus Christ. Not only had we met a very kind, compassionate doctor, but we had met a brother in Christ.

We left there in joy and I came back home to my normal life.

At almost the same time that I had experienced the health problems that had begun my journey, one of my friends experienced the exact same symptoms.

But her news was not the same. Her news didn't bring her back to her normal life. Her news began a new kind of life. She wasn't able to catch her breath until she took her last breath here and her next breath in heaven.

As you read this you can see that my story turned out not to be much of a story. Oh, I can play the brain tumor card at family gatherings when I don't want to help with the dishes. I can pull it out if there is an event I don't want to attend. You know, *"I really shouldn't do that. After all, I do have a brain tumor!"* But I am going to be very honest that line didn't have much of a shelf life.

So why did God walk me down the valley of the shadow of death, only to lift me out so quickly?

There are a number of reasons but the one that tops the list is the opportunity to share the good news with people that no matter what we face, Jesus can walk us through it.

A teacher once told his students that they must

repent one day before they die. That certainly begged the question: *"So, will we know when we will die?"* *"No."* He responded. *"Repent today!"*

One day we each will take our last breath here and catch our next breath in eternity.

You can know for sure that that breath will be in heaven. The Bible outlines for us that there is some bad news, some really bad news, some hopeful news and some great news.

Here is the bad news:
We are all sinners.

Here is the really bad news:
Our sin separates us from God and the result is that we are headed for a place called hell.

Here is the hopeful news:
Jesus loves us so much that He came into this world to lift our sin from us and carry it to a cross where His blood could wash it away forever. It is the greatest gift ever offered.

Here is the great news:
We can receive that gift by praying a very simple prayer that can go something like this:

Dear Jesus,

*I know the Bible says that I am a sinner. I am
sorry for my sins and ask you to come into my life
to forgive me of my sins and make me your child.
I accept you as my Lord, my Savior and my very
best Friend.*

*Thank you for dying for me. Help me to live for you.
Thank you. In Jesus' name I pray.*

Amen

One day I will stare death in the face and I know who
will blink first. I will. But the next catch of my breath
will mean I am staring into the very eyes of Jesus...
never to blink again!

Genesis 1

"And God saw all that He had made and it was very good." Genesis 1:31

What a privilege that He also allows us to see, hear, taste, feel, experience all that He has made. Today we just want to take a few minutes to say *"thank you."*

Thank You Lord for all that I get to see, my husband, children, and grandchildren's faces, the sun coming up each morning and setting at night, the colors of a rainbow, crimson, golden, flaming orange leaves falling, snowcapped mountains and vast oceans. Sometimes I feel as if I can't look enough, some views so breathtaking that it hurts.

Thank You for all the sounds I hear, the laughter of my babies, the words *"I love you"*, a friend's voice on the phone, music that floods my soul. Thank You for the millions of sounds that fill my heart with so much joy that it hurts.

Thank You for allowing me a heart to love and be loved. Thank You for the feeling of snowflakes on my face and the warmth of the sun. Thank You for days that can be spent outside and days at home by the fire. Thank You for family meals, sometimes the small family and sometimes so many that we're sitting on the floor.

Thank You for health, or walking with me when I'm not so healthy.

Thank You for special, wonderful days like Christmas, days we plan for and anticipate and look forward to. And thank You for ordinary days that can become extraordinary days.

Thank You for chocolate, and practical things like aluminum foil and plastic wrap.

Thank You for the sweetness of Your Word that draws me near to You. Thank You for coming to save me. Father, what I know, what I see, what I hear, what I experience all tell me that Your Word is absolutely true. All that You made is so very good because You are so very good.

Thank You is not enough.

Day 17

I know what it means to grow up a multiple. I did not know what it meant to help care for multiples.

My daughter went to have a routine ultra sound. Her husband was working so I went along to hold her son while the technician did the procedure. I could sit in if I wanted. *"Of course!"*

The tech asked why she was there. My daughter informed her that she just needed an idea of how far along she was. I jokingly said I wanted to know if it was a multiple birth. With all the children my sisters, brothers and I have had, seventeen in all, there had not been a single set of twins.

Now, with this next generation, this was the twenty-fifth time one of those kids had been expecting. It seemed no one was going to have a multiple birth. The tech just laughed, *"Well, I doubt it's twins."* She began the procedure, then paused and cleared her throat. *"I guess I lied, there ARE two babies."*

And I could see. Two tiny babies. Twins. My daughter started to cry, not just out of joy, but also out of fear. *"No, no, the Doctor heard just one heartbeat!"* (that in sync thing again).

But *"Yes. Yes!"* They were twins, two gorgeous baby girls. They arrived and then lived behind closed doors for two weeks in the NICU where only Mommy and Daddy got to view them and hold then and kiss their sweet faces. Then they came home to be cared for by mom and dad and anyone else who could help. I always thought twins would be twice the work. They aren't. They are about four times the work. They don't call them multiples for nothing. Everything is multiplied. The work, the lack of sleep, the diapers, and these are disposable. How many diapers can someone change in a five-minute time frame? When one was sleeping, the other was crying. No rest, no sleep, and I am just the grandmother. How long can parents survive without sleep? But survive they did and the result is more than quadruple the fun. They are exquisite, fabulous bundles of energy and love, soooo worth the no rest.

You know, God knew we needed rest. He knew we needed sleep. When we don't get it, life is hard. He built it into the core of our fabric. Sleep at night and a Sabbath for rest. When we awake each morning, it's a new beginning. When we start each week, it's a new beginning. And that really is a gift right from the heart of God.

Genesis 2

Genesis 2:1-3. *"Thus the heavens and the earth were completed in all their vast array. By the seventh day God had finished the work He had been doing; so on the seventh day He rested from all His work. Then God blessed the seventh day and made it holy, because on it He rested from all the work of creating that He had done."*

First, the gift of creation and all the beauty, the wonder, the detail and the splendor that it entails and then...the gift of rest. It wasn't that God grew tired; He never slumbers or sleeps. It wasn't that God needed to take a break to renew His creative power. He is Elohim, the Creator God. It was that He was finished. Every bit of the creation was complete. Every tiny detail was done. And so He rested from the work and gave us the gift of resting from our work.

I have to wonder if at that moment, the words, *"It is finished"* rang through the universe.

We don't know, but we do know that a day was coming when the voice of God would cry out, *"It is finished"*, because there on a wooden cross every bit of the re-creation process would be completed. Every detail fulfilled, every bit of the work needed to redeem us, to make us a new creation was accomplished. Jesus did it all. He gave us the gift of rest from working for our salvation. There is not one thing we need do to earn it. There is nothing we must accomplish to be worthy of it. He gave the gift of salvation and all that it entails and also...the gift of rest. We just need to receive it.

"It is finished!"...some of the most beautiful words ever spoken.

Day 18

Cardiopulmonary resuscitation includes chest compressions and rescue breathing. I've never had to use CPR or even seen it used in real life to save the life of a real person. I hope I never do. I absolutely don't want to be in a situation where someone is in that much danger and counting on me.

Medical stuff is not my thing. We come from a long line of fainters. Mom was a nurse; Dad wasn't. The sight of meat blood was okay but one drop of human blood and Dad was on the floor.

One Sunday morning our pastor started talking about an injury he had gotten while putting up his Christmas tree. Most of the time erecting a Christmas tree does not involve the shedding of blood, but the details were just a little too graphic and our brother had to leave the service. He made it out, but barely before the blackness rising from the floor hit his eyes.

Kris gets light headed just talking about pierced ears.

At the birth of my third child a nurse came into the room to get me up. But somehow she read the family heritage on my face. She asked, *"Are you a fainter? 'Cause ya look like a fainter."*

I lived up to her words.

We went into education for a reason.

But I want to be prepared so I've taken the classes and practiced on a dummy (not a real person). I do know how it works. The breathing from the one helps to restore the breath of the other. CPR is up close and personal, but sometimes critically necessary to save a life.

I think, I hope, I PRAY (and believe me, I would be praying) that if called upon I could rise to the occasion. But this one thing I know: if I ever have to use it, afterward someone had better be prepared to use CPR on me.

Genesis 2

In chapter 2 of Genesis we get a little closer look at the creation of man. God spoke and the rest of creation appeared. But for the man, God formed him from the dust of the earth.

Dirt. It seems appropriate that people are made from dirt, clay, mud, dust, soil, sand, a variety of shades of color. Loving gentle hands shaped the man. The very ground we walk on became his body. And then, the God of all creation bent down and breathed one breath of His Eternal Life into that lifeless body and man became a living being. This is up close, intimate, personal, the mighty God, kneeling in front of His creation, lovingly placing His face as close as a whisper and giving His Life to the man.

On another day, on a dirty hillside, the living God would exhale and with His last breath give His life for man. Man was born and can be born again out of that love, that care, that close personal encounter with our God. And God has never moved. He is still today no farther than a whisper. And that is the closeness, the intimate personal relationship He wants to have with His creation still today, right here, right now.

"...the Lord God formed the man from the dust of the ground and breathed into his nostrils the breath of life and the man became a living being."
Genesis 2:7

Day 19

Makeup, I started to wear it in my teenage years. Oh it wasn't a lot, just enough to make up for what I didn't naturally have, a little rosier cheeks, a little pinker smile. Any makeup worked, the cheap over the counter stuff that didn't require a bank loan to buy, just plain makeup.

After about a decade of the ordinary stuff I found that a change was in order. I started using brands that didn't just say makeup. Now I leaned toward those brands that had the word *"enhancing"* in their name. I no longer just needed to make up for what I didn't have; I also needed to make the most of what I did have. Enlarge the eyes, lengthen the lashes, heighten the cheekbones. It was a time consuming venture.

Then came the cover up years. Make up for, enhance what you have, and apply a cover of serious makeup over the rest. Wrinkles would disappear. Laugh lines fade into oblivion. This would cover over and escort me right into the look of the air brushed models. The home shopping network carried products that promised to cover without anyone even suspecting that you were wearing a thick layer of makeup. It looked soooo natural...on TV. And it would enhance what you have and make up for what you don't and create beauty, and stop world hunger and deliver world peace. Seriously, this product worked. It worked on TV. One product for the *"low, low"* price of the down payment on a house. But you know, soooooooooo worth it 'cause the world would not see a wrinkle and of course that world peace thing.

And then I discovered the age defying stuff. Really, now this was what I was waiting for. These little miracles would take a stand for me against the aging process. While I slept, when I worked, while I cooked and cleaned and the days slipped by, they would do their anti-aging thing and time would stop and no part of my face would ever wrinkle or sag or droop ever again. If I just bought this or that product, time would reverse itself, youth would return. Can I just say it is wonderful to live in a time and place where so many amazing cosmetics work tirelessly to make my face something people are not terrified to see.

Thirty-eight years ago at our grandmother's funeral, lots of people came and went. They offered their condolences. To be honest I don't remember too much of what was said, except for this one statement. Someone walked up to me at Grandma's funeral and told me, *"I have never seen your grandmother look better."*

"Never"? This person had NEVER seen my Grandma

look better? Did you catch that this was my grandmother's funeral and she had *"never looked better"*?

My first thought was that I always thought Grandma looked better alive.

I didn't know how to answer, *"Ummm... thanks?"* Or, *"Yeah, you're right. I'm really hoping I look that good at my funeral."*

Now all these years later I've started wondering just where one goes to buy beauty products that promise death-defying results.

I'm thinking it just might be time for me to buy some of those.

But no matter how good makeup can make someone look, even if it works to put a healthy glow on a death pallor, even if it is the best someone ever looked, dead is still dead.

And with death comes the question, *"What happens when we die?"*

Genesis 2

What happens when we die? Some would say that it is the end, that man returns to the state of nothingness in which he existed before he was born. And thus, they are staking their eternal destiny on that thought, that they will just cease to be.

But God says that we have the breath of the Eternal God in us.

Genesis 2:7 tells us *"Then the Lord God formed a man from the dust of the ground and breathed into his nostrils the breath of life, and the man became a living being."*

One breath from the God who was, who is, and who will forever be, and thus, we have an eternal destiny. The life that He gave to us will never cease. Our bodies die, they are but dust. But the real person that we are, will continue. We will exist somewhere.

The Bible says there are two choices...heaven or hell. But why would a loving God make a place like hell? Because He is loving and love doesn't force anyone to love in return.

Love doesn't demand that we choose His presence. Hell is the place of God's absence.

He is the firm foundation. If God isn't there, there is no foundation, only a bottomless pit.

God is peace. If that peace is missing, what is left is torment.

Jesus is the living water. Apart from Him there is unquenchable thirst.

He is the light. All of heaven is lit by His brightness. Hell is a place of total darkness because He is not there.

We have in us the breath of the eternal, and so we will continue to be. He is Eternal Life, apart from Him there is only eternal death.

The choice is ours.

Day 20

We already told you that our parents put out a BIG garden. We planted every vegetable known to man. From A-Z, asparagus to zucchini, if the seed catalogue carried it, I think we tried it.

As kids we wanted to play, but gardening came first. We would plant, weed, hoe, reap, and then if the planting, hoeing, weeding, and reaping weren't fun enough, there was the job of picking fat creepy tomato worms off the plants to keep them from eating the fruit. And then there was the removal of the potato bugs to keep them from destroying the plants.

Seriously it was the stuff of nightmares. God knew we needed brothers. They weren't as creeped out by those pests.

If it got dry, we hauled water from the creek. It took a lot of work to insure a crop. Weeds crept in overnight. Morning glories are lovely to look at in your flower garden, but dreadful in a vegetable garden. Their creeping crawling vines choked out the vegetables. Thistles, they too have a beautiful flower, but removing them meant tiny sharp needles sticking into your hands. Gloves? Who knew?

And then the lima beans and peas all had to be picked, shelled, washed, and frozen for the winter. The corn needed husking, its silky hair-like tassels removed and then all the kernels cut off so it could be frozen. A billion (yes, we counted) tomatoes had to be washed. Prickly little cucumbers were scrubbed to remove the prickles and then they became sweet and dill pickles. Green beans were snapped, the ends removed, cleaned, then canned or frozen. Potatoes were dug, it's a little like finding buried treasure, a very little, and the potatoes stored for the winter. Lettuce and spinach triple washed to remove any tiny critters hanging on.

The garden was a lot of WORK, TOIL, SWEAT.

Need I say, none of the six of us have vegetable gardens today. I for one am very grateful for farmer's markets.

Genesis 2

In Genesis 2:8-9 it says, *"Now the Lord God had planted a garden in the east, in Eden; and there He put the man He had formed. The Lord God made all kinds of trees grow out of the ground-trees that were pleasing to the eye and good for food. In the middle of the garden were the tree of life and the tree of the knowledge of good and evil."*

When God planted His garden in Eden and placed the man there to work the garden, it wasn't the same kind of work. NO WEEDS! Just lush growth, beauty in the variety, the ground was perfectly watered. No bugs attacked the plants. Flowers and fruits and vegetables that were pleasing to the eye and wonderful to eat, grew abundantly. It was paradise.

In the middle of the garden were the tree of life and the tree of the knowledge of good and evil, two trees that presented a choice. To choose the one meant death, to choose the other meant life.

It seems a simple choice.

But we have the same choice today. We can eat from the tree that the world offers or we can choose the tree that leads to Life.

It seems a simple choice.

Day 21

I've been single for a long time now. What I've found is that after I healed from the trauma of that broken relationship, I eventually began to wonder about a new relationship. But even though sometimes it's kind of lonely, honestly, the alternative leaves a lot to be desired. I'm not talking about marriage. I'm not one bit jaded about that.

What I'm talking about is dating. UGHHH. I will have to admit I've not had too much practice. It seems that most of the time I can only get through initial meetings. Maybe there's a reason for that.

One man came into town on a business trip. I met him for dinner a couple of times during that initial contact. I thought we were beginning a friendship. He thought I belonged to him. After he left he made about 300 phone calls asking me what I was doing. Later a huge box was delivered to my home filled with clothes, books, and a $400.00 cell phone that was already programmed with his number. He said he would pay for the phone. At first glance that sounds just lovely. But my son-in-law pointed out to me that he then could track everyone I called.

I boxed everything right back up and sent it back. I didn't want to be tracked. I think his last name was STALKER.

I talked with another man for a few weeks and we decided to meet. He came with gifts. I had told him to absolutely not do that because of the other situation. He did it anyway. It should have been a clue. He started talking about good news. When I hear the term *"good news"* I think about something relating to the Scripture. He had another idea. I asked him what the good news was. He said he was going to sell his business and move here. He was sure I would welcome him in MY home. (Now remember this was the very first time I had ever even met this man.)

I swallowed a couple of times and excused myself. I went into the bathroom and looked at myself in the mirror wiping my face with a wet towel. I kept asking what on earth I had said that could somehow be misconstrued to that. I went back out and as clearly, distinctively, and forcefully said, *"I believe we are not at all on the same page! I came to meet a friend, you came to claim a wife."*

I LEFT!

Another man wanted to see a picture of me. I hate pictures. They are one moment frozen in time and not nearly the complexity of who I am. Besides

I had not yet learned the art of *"squinching"* my eyes, which I am told, makes every picture perfect. But I sent him one anyway and this is (it is verbatim, I kept it) what he said:

"What I am about to suggest may end our conversations and contact, but I will offer it as a Christian brother, and a marketing man. I think that you can do better in marketing yourself. Lose the glasses, they make you look 'frumpy.' Either get a newer, more stylish pair or consider contacts, perhaps even laser surgery if possible...Those frames simply don't do much for the shape of your face. The colors you were wearing don't seem best for you. If you have never had a personal consultation with a female image consultant, do it now! If you need money for this, tell your kids and friends to chip in for the 'Let's Rehab Kathie Project.' Don't be bashful, do it! Review your entire wardrobe if need be, but get help from someone knowledgeable and honest. Next get to the hairstylist. That look is like something from the '60's and the "hootenannies" or the movie, "Pleasantville." Last of all, get help with makeup. I may be wrong, but I get the impression that you have not had a consultation with an excellent cosmetologist."

Hard to believe this guy was single. He never even made it to a first meeting.

Although I know that God said *"It is not good for a man (and by default, a woman) to be alone"*, I have decided that He is going to have to be the One who makes that happen for me. I'm not at all worried about my future. God has it and, if it would be part of His divine plan, that special *"him"* in His hands as well.

Genesis 2

*"The Lord God said, 'It is not good for the man to
be alone. I will make a helper suitable for him'."*
Genesis 2:18

Everything that God had created He said was
good. The word good is a big word, it entails a
lot. It means good, pleasant, beautiful, excellent,
lovely, delightful, joyful, fruitful, precious, well,
you get the point...a big word.

But this aloneness was not good. Adam's position
of being the only human was not going to
encompass all of the blissful state that God
intended. I think God wanted Adam to recognize
even in the beautiful, perfect garden, that there
was more that God wanted to give him, more
that God wanted to bless him with. God brought
the animals, and as magnificent as they were, as
Adam named each one, he recognized that not
one was a suitable mate for him.

So God performed surgery. He put Adam to sleep,
removed his rib and fashioned a woman. Literally, she
was made for him and they were indeed one flesh.

The man, the woman, God's wonderful gift and
this was so beautiful, excellent, pleasant, lovely,
delightful... you get the point. This was very good.

Day 22

Weddings are lovely occasions. The groom anxiously awaits at the end of an aisle for his bride. It is a heart stirring moment when you see his face light as she comes into view and begins to make her way toward him. It's an intimate glimpse of the love they share, which can not only be seen, but almost felt as you behold their faces. We, the wedding guests, get to witness this. It is a picture of pure joy.

But then life happens and joy is sometimes turned into great sadness. Promises that were made publicly are broken in secret. Divorce is awful. It's like getting cut in half with a dull knife and then, with the even duller side of the blade, having your insides scraped out. It takes a long time to recover. When you're in so much pain, you need healing.

I did find it.

I had for years read my Bible daily. It was part of my normal routine. I taught Sunday School and Bible classes so I had studied. But when you feel like you have fallen over a cliff, you have to have something to hold onto. God's Word is that strong, triple-braided rope that will NOT let you go if you grab on. I began to sleep with my Bible right next to me. In the middle of the night when I would wake up with a jolt, hoping, praying that what I was living was a nightmare, I would read. I would read until I was so sleepy it would often slip out of my hands, opened on my chest, as I went back to sleep.

Early in the morning, I would reopen its pages and take in its words until I could feel the peace flow into my weary, hurting heart. It brought strength to me so I could face the day.

Sometimes when I would get home from work, I would read again because coming home to emptiness was hard to face and the words would fill that void.

Often, when it was laying there beside me at night, as I was trying to quiet the voices of fear, and doubt, and the feelings of being unloved, I would grab it and read some more.

There were times when my heart was filled with so much sadness that I couldn't formulate words to pray. So I prayed the Psalms. I would read them over and over again. The love of God's sweet Word would overpower me and often I would close the Book and hold it close to my heart. It was more than reading, it was more than studying. I began to just love what He had to say to me.

You see on every page I met the One who loves me

more than any human ever could. I saw on every page a Bridegroom who would always be faithful and true. His promises would never be broken.

A love, a dependency for God's Word has changed my life. Studying became more than just looking at one text. It became instead a treasure hunt. I found that sometimes words were connected in other Scriptures and I would begin to follow that path. I started looking at what the words meant as I studied verses that spoke to me. I began to look at the names and what those names meant. It's amazing what happens when we begin to dig for the treasure buried not only in the text but within it. I realized that every word, every name, every date, every letter was there on purpose. It was and is delightful.

Is there a part of me that is saddened that I do not have a husband? The answer to that is yes. I would love to experience what true, faithful love is like between a man and a woman. But I know that there is coming a day when THE BRIDEGROOM'S face will light as I come into view and He will never leave, never forsake and will carry me over the threshold of my eternal home. He is the ONE who meets me on every page of His Book, for He is the Word of God.

The countdown to that wedding has already begun.

Genesis 2

The Garden, the perfect place, God put Adam there after his creation. This garden would have electrified the senses, and satisfied the soul. But all of it wasn't yet enough. God had more for Adam, the beautiful gift of marriage. Adam saw the animals, and not one was right.

"So the Lord God caused the man to fall into a deep sleep; and while he was sleeping, He took one of the man's ribs and then closed up the place with flesh. Then the Lord God made a woman from the rib He had taken out of the man, and He brought her to the man.

The man said, 'for she shall be called woman, for she was taken out of man.' That is why a man leaves his father and mother and is united to his wife, and they become one flesh." Genesis 2:21-24

God put him to sleep, a deep sleep, and the bride was formed out of Adam's side. Eve had to have been exquisite, God's perfect creation and perfectly suited just for Adam. Adam did nothing to earn this gift, or to deserve it.

It was simply born out of God's loving heart.

Our world is a magnificent place, though no longer perfect. It can be soul stirring and exhilarating. It can electrify the senses.

But that is not enough. God created us for relationship, not just with a spouse, but with Him. Jesus died, the ultimate sleep, and the bride was formed out of His wounded side.

We aren't so exquisite, definitely not perfect, and there's not a thing we can do to earn or deserve His gift.

It was simply born out of God's loving heart.

Day 23

As we said we have two (they would point out MUCH) younger brothers. Both are great men of faith and integrity. But though they are truly good men, neither is perfect. The one, who is closest to my age, was often times my hero. He was the one who would come to my rescue if I went wading in our creek and came out attacked by giant leaches, seriously they lived there. He bravely wrangled the tomato worms when we girls were terrified to touch them. He is the one of whom legendary stories are told to my students when I see that my teaching on *"how to write a literary analysis"* is putting them to sleep. He has become Super Dan. He could lift grandma and grandpa's gigantic bull with one finger, He could leap tall buildings with a single bound. He was faster than a speeding bullet...oh wait that's not Super Dan, that's Superman, but regardless, I pull up a stool and begin a story from my childhood that usually involves my brother. This is one I have told. It is a story about food, and a very bad choice.

It was a Wednesday. Mother helped Dad at the grocery store meat department on Wednesdays because it was his assistant's day off. So when we got home that afternoon we had responsibilities that went beyond the norm. Dan was in sixth grade and

Bill was about six. We were supposed to get supper started and Dan was supposed to work in the yard.

When we got home from school we were like most kids, ravenous. We were ready to eat almost anything that was not nailed down. So we grabbed a snack and headed upstairs to change our clothes so we could do what we were supposed to do.

At this point in the story I'm sure you can see the halos, but actually we were too afraid of Dad's displeasure to do anything else. If we didn't do what we were supposed to do there were consequences. The consequences were cleaning up around the trees in the yard with a hoe and rake. We lived on three acres of woods that dad had cleared just to build the house. Believe me making dinner in a timely fashion was far preferable to that.

But Dan got side tracked from his chores. He needed a snack and couldn't decide what to choose. So like many kids he began to study the refrigerator contents.

Now let me also explain the logistics of the refrigerator. For some reason, unknown to me, our fridge was on a bit of a shelf about six inches off the floor. Perhaps that helped if there was water leakage. Maybe it made the kitchen look better. I just don't know, but that's how it was. Dan couldn't see well enough into both sides of the side-by-side refrigerator-freezer so he manipulated his feet onto the ledge. There was not nearly enough room, so in order to steady himself and still be able to scan, he held onto both sides of the top of the massive avocado appliance.

Then as he studied, surveying and contemplating his options, he began to relax. As he relaxed, he began to lean backwards ever so slightly, still with his hands gripping the sides for balance and support until he realized he was moving toward a prone position and so was the refrigerator.

Suddenly he became aware that this huge thing was falling forward and was going to crush him if he didn't react. With one burst of supernatural, superhero strength he pushed himself back up and managed to save the refrigerator from crashing onto his then about ninety pound frame.

Now I don't know a great deal about physics but there are some laws of motion that I do know. One is that when an object is set in motion it continues to stay in motion unless it is met with an equal or greater force. Dan's super strength equaled the force of the refrigerator, managing to push it back into its place but what he did not reckon on was that the items in the refrigerator had no such force. Suddenly all those things that had been stored on the shelves were free and moving.

Here I should also add that this took place in the early 1960's, long before most items came in plastic bottles. Almost every food item was manufactured in glass back then. Ketchup, mustard, pickles, milk, gallons of milk, enough for a family of six kids, mayonnaise and any other store-bought condiment was housed in a breakable container. Along with these glass items came several dozen eggs. Grandma had a chicken farm so eggs were in abundance at our house and although stored in cardboard they hit the floor on top of the crashing glass.

As I said, my sisters and I were upstairs. I have no real words to describe the sound except it has to be comparable to the heart stopping crash of a vehicle collision. I heard it, the reverberating sound of glass crunching against glass, but my mind couldn't grasp what on earth inside the house could have made that sound. I ran to where the noise was coming from and what I found was nothing short of disastrous. The sight of glass, lots of glass, chards of glass, scattered and broken, mingled with ketchup, mustard, mayonnaise, pickles, milk and eggs splattered everywhere in the kitchen, was unbelievable.

Several years ago there was a commercial on TV, which showed a refrigerator being tipped and the mess it made. This ad was for paper towels. Let me be the first to say there is not a paper towel alive that could have dealt with this mess. It was unspeakable.

And Dan? Well Dan had chores to do so off he went to do them, leaving the screen door swinging and my sisters and me to deal with his mess. I wanted to go after him but knew that my mother would soon be home and the thought of her seeing this and bursting into tears was too much. I knew it had to be taken care of first. So we cleaned it up. I believe we used a shovel. It was honestly the biggest mess I have ever seen inside a house.

Did our parents ever find out? Duhhhh! We were two years older than Dan so of course it was our duty, our joy, to tell on him. Besides there had to be an explanation for no food in the refrigerator. His punishment was not nearly severe enough. But let it suffice to say that the trees were perfectly manicured that summer and he was grateful it was a stand up job.

One choice can really make a mess.

Genesis 2

"And the Lord God commanded the man, 'You are free to eat from any tree in the garden; but you must not eat from the tree of the knowledge of good and evil, for when you eat from it you will surely die.'" Genesis 2:16-17

God's Word to Adam was that he was free to eat from all of the trees in the garden except the tree of the knowledge of good and evil. One tree in the middle of the garden was forbidden. One tree and only one, but Satan came to Eve to try to distort God's truth.

Genesis 3:1, *"Now the serpent was more crafty than any of the wild animals the Lord God had made. He said to the woman, 'Did God really say, 'You must not eat from any tree in the garden'?"*

Satan, in the guise of the serpent, came to Eve. In a few short words he spoke the same subtle lies that he still whispers to people today. The first lie, *"Did God really say?"* Satan was planting doubt about the truth of God's Word. Such a lie. If we examine the Scripture, as we look closely, we discover that it is absolutely true.

The second lie, *"You must not eat from ANY tree in the garden."* Satan wanted her to believe that God was holding out on her, that God had created lots of great things but she couldn't partake of them.

Knowing God isn't bondage, it is freedom. A relationship with God doesn't limit our lives; it leads to the biggest life possible.

One choice can really make a mess.

Day 24

I saw a T-shirt once that had a message that went something like this: *"If we were meant to be vegetarians, it would be more fun to shoot broccoli."*

There are hunters in my family and there are Bambi lovers, so I am not getting into a gun debate. But I am going to tell a gun story.

All four of us sisters were in a car accident. We were not left with life threatening injuries but we were pretty banged up.

A couple of us had gaping cuts across our foreheads that ended up giving us faces that looked like raccoons. I had a pretty severe concussion and we were advised that I should stay the night in the hospital. But I wouldn't hear of it. My hard head was screaming so loudly and the message it was rapping to me was: *"I just want to go home!"*

My resolve met the doctor's and for some reason he caved and let me have my way.

This accident happened about 70 miles from home, so it was a pretty uncomfortable journey. I wavered between sleep and nausea.

It was a night to try to forget but became a night to remember.

We got home and got settled in bed. Our mom was hovering but as soon as our dad saw that we were nestled all snug in our beds...albeit, not in a kerchief, but rather in layers of bandages wrapped around our blood-soaked heads, he went downstairs.

Our dad is not a blood lover and he needed to leave the room. He passed out once getting his blood pressure taken. I guess the pressure was too much for him. Besides he had a mission and was on his way to accomplish it.

We lived on a three-acre, park-like, forest-lawn stretch of property out in the country. We had neighbors within a stone's throw but not in spitting distance. So we were out there.

Our dad had been told by some of the neighbors that property was being vandalized in the area and he wanted to make sure that our house and shed were safe.

He had an old rifle and a few bullets. Dad only wanted to make some noise with it and scare off any potential hooligans before they even set foot on our back-forty, well, okay back-three.

He had the strategy and was getting everything

ready. The weapons that we usually used around our home were shovels and rakes to ward off weeds. But our dad had grown up in an era when it was not a bit unusual for a farmer to keep a gun. Our mom told me not long ago that as a girl she was known to hunt groundhogs for supper. I don't think we ever ate that but there maybe were a few suppers that felt like we were eating mystery meat. (Wait, maybe that was my cooking!) But really, she was such a good cook, she could have made cardboard taste good. (I simply did not spend enough time with Mom in the kitchen. I was probably studying. Okay, watching TV.)

So Dad knew his way around guns and was simply preparing to make some noise.

And he did.

I was just ready to nod off into unconscious land when I heard a shot...followed by an explosion. My mom raced to the stairs and called my dad's name.

Nothing. No response. I couldn't even catch my breath. A shot? An explosion?

She flew down the steps.

She got to the family room. There was Dad. He stood there with the gun pointing to the floor, a way more than sheepish look on his face. The only words that he could utter were *"Aw, nuts!"*

Our dad had shot and killed the TV. Even our mom was not going to be able to turn that *"kill"* into mystery meat.

Years later Linda went into a local TV repair shop to get some advice. Somehow the conversation turned to the worst repair job he had ever been asked to do. You guessed it. He told her about a guy who had shot his TV.

When I heard what had happened, I finally could catch a breath but then I collapsed. That night was so tension-filled, hurt-filled and fear-filled that I just wanted to become Rip Van Winkle and sleep for the next twenty years.

Genesis 3

Do you know what I've learned? I have learned that sometimes in this world, we get hurt. I have been hurt several times in the past few years. These have not been little wounds. I had not seen them coming and I had the wind knocked out of me. I went to the Lord and almost shouted, *"This is not fair! I don't deserve this!"*

And do you know what? That is absolutely true. I don't deserve this. I deserve far worse. In reality I deserve hell and nothing better!

Sometimes, it is those we love or those we call our friends, that hurt us the deepest or the most often. But why would I even begin to think that that should never happen to me?

I know this: I am a sinner and I live in a world of sinners. We hurt each other. Sometimes a shot is fired and it is more than a TV that explodes.

Let's make this completely clear. Satan doesn't just hate God's creation, Satan hates God. *"Now the serpent was more crafty than any of the wild animals the Lord God had made. He said to the woman, 'Did God really say, 'You must not eat from any tree from the garden?'"*

Satan wasn't just asking a question. His design

was to lead them astray. The temptation of Adam and Eve was to separate them from God, hurt God's creation and wound God's heart.

The temptation is not any different today. It is designed to separate us from God, hurt God's creation and wound God's heart.

That means we get hurt and I'm not talking about just car accidents.

So let me turn the conversation back to the question. What is the worst repair job that was ever asked to be done?

Answer? It was a broken world.

How was it repaired? Jesus went to the cross.

Day 25

There is something I need to admit. I had never understood why Adam and Eve, especially Eve, disobeyed God so easily. They had the perfect marriage, the perfect home, the perfect relationship with God. They had it all, it was perfect. They weren't even hungry. But yet, they disobeyed.

God told Adam not to eat from the tree of the knowledge of good and evil. Who told Eve? Did God? Or was it Adam? It seems more likely it was Adam. He was to protect and care for Eve. As parents, when we don't want our children to break something we say, *"Don't even touch it"*. Did Adam say that to Eve? God never told Adam not to touch it. But here was Eve carrying on a conversation with Satan about this tree and she added that they were not to touch it.

Regardless of where that information came from, it is great advice. She should have listened to her own advice. JUST DON'T TOUCH.

I have something else to admit. There are times I watch home shopping channels on television. I have learned some of the hosts and hostesses whom I feel I can trust more than others. The reason I watch is simply this, my husband and I have Christmas gifts to buy for people who seem to have everything. Okay, I confess sometimes I will buy that especially needed gift for me. Last year I bought something for my sister-in-law and she still talks about it. You can buy basically anything from home shopping. There are decorating shows, kitchen shows, jewelry shows, shows for men, shows for grandkids, electronic shows, makeup shows, furniture shows, fashion shows - you name it, there is a show.

On one particular day I was watching a fashion show. (When I say I watch I mean I am sipping coffee, cooking, reading, cleaning, doing a myriad of things all while home shopping is in the background.) There was a guest on this show, a television star, selling her line of fashions. The guest hostess and the regular hostess were oohing and awing over all the lovely creations. But nothing had really piqued my interest to purchase as that special gift for someone else or even for myself.

And then the next product came on. I almost spewed out my coffee. Part of this fashion experience included a TURBAN. Now, I suppose there is a place for fashionable turbans, but not in HIGH fashion. This was not just any old turban not just that subtle hat that looks so adorable making others envious of your turban. The material in this one went in a criss cross pattern across the front. It was so tall you could carry your lunch inside of it. Now, I know we would all like to look taller, taller from the waist down, but not from the forehead up. They came in a virtual plethora of very bright colors.

Suddenly I was thinking that I could just put a neon light on my head that goes round and round or maybe a loud speaker that says *"I have a turban and you don't have one."*

So my next thought was, *"Come on, move it along, who would buy this?"*

But. . . the more she spoke, the more I listened. A turban actually started to make sense. I could wear it on a bad hair day. If the weather was bad, I could pull it on my head and go. Of course I would have to keep it on all day because I would have turban hair if I took it off. I could leave it by the front door and put it on if someone came unexpectedly. At any moment of any day, I could leave at a moment's notice wearing my brightly colored turban.

This made sense! This was good! This WAS HIGH FASHION! I would be the bell of the ball with my turban! People would soon be asking me *"Where did you get that turban? I have been looking for one just like that my whole life."*

Quickly, I dialed the number because by this time I had it memorized. What if the line was busy? What if I couldn't get through? I kept fearing that the hostess might say they were all sold out. I was becoming frantic. I might not be able to purchase this much needed turban. But then...relief, the phone was ringing. I was actually getting through.

And then suddenly a moment of clarity, I realized I WAS BUYING A TURBAN. A TURBAN! I NEVER WEAR TURBANS. I DO NOT EVEN WEAR HATS!!!!!!!! Can you hear me screaming this? I hung up the phone. I did not purchase a turban that day. It would not have been that special gift for any of the women in my life. It would never have worked for me because I never have, nor ever will wear a brightly colored turban that sits high on my head.

I get it Eve. As wrong as it was, and wow, it was wrong. Satan made it sound so wonderful. Sin can be subtle, intriguing, enticing and fun. It can make sense to you. You can look at it first and think it's wrong, but the more you listen, the more you are faced with it, the more you begin to justify it, then you embrace it.

Here is what I have learned from Eve.

When enticed DO NOT:
look
listen
touch
justify
embrace

DO:
pray
seek the truth of God's Word.

Eve should have run to God. So should we!

Genesis 3, Psalm 104

When God created Adam and Eve, the Bible says they were naked and unashamed. No sin, no shame, nothing impure or unclean about them. Purity, innocence reigned in the garden. But Satan came with his temptation and Eve looked at the fruit. Oh, it looked good. It was good for food, pleasing to the eye, and it would make her wise.

So she took some and ate it. She also gave some to Adam and he ate it. The moment they ate, they knew.

They knew that they had disobeyed God.

They knew that they had sinned.

They knew that they were naked and now they needed a covering.

So what changed? I believe, that in the garden, Adam and Eve were surrounded by God's Glory. The light of His Presence was their covering. Psalm 104:2 says, *"He wraps Himself in light as with a garment."*

I think that's how Adam and Eve lived before they sinned. But God's Presence, His Shekinah Glory, won't dwell with sin, so as soon as they disobeyed, God's glorious light was removed and they knew it. Now, nakedness made them exposed, uncomfortable, shame reigned in the garden. They now knew too well the difference between good and evil. Their eyes were indeed opened, just not in the way they had anticipated.

Day 26

A few years ago one of my sons-in-law needed
to go out of the country to work on perfecting
a technique he was going to use in his practice.
Since he was going to be busy four days of each of
the three weeks he was there, that would have left
my daughter with large chunks of time running
around Frankfort, Germany, alone. They asked me
to go along. Chance to travel to Europe? Uhhh...a
resounding, *"YES!"* He was a student, she was
not working, and I live on a teacher's salary so we
made the trip as economically as possible. Nothing
fancy, but still, it was Europe. (Several years before
that I had been sure my life was over and there
would never be anything sweet or lovely again. I
was so very wrong. God is the author of big and
lovely and delightful and this was all of those.)

So we went. Economical meant lots of walking, but
in Frankfort that was common. Most people walk,
ride bikes, take buses or trains. We fit in very well
except for the whole cameras hanging around our
necks and passport holders hidden badly under
our shirts.

One morning my daughter and I went out walking.
It was early so not many shops were yet open,
but the streets were beautiful, with almost every

window adorned with boxes of flowers cascading over them. That year Germany was unusually hot. People in Europe don't value air conditioning quite as much as we do, so almost everywhere we went was hot. It was hot that morning. But we loved being out, exploring the wonders of Frankfort.

As we walked, suddenly I had the sense that someone was approaching us. You know how you can feel that? I turned around. What I saw made me react quickly, spontaneously, to protect my daughter. (It's kind of like when driving if you have to stop too quickly you instantly throw out your right arm to try to protect whoever is sitting in the passenger seat.) That was my reaction.

What did I see?

A man.

A man, and he was naked, completely, not one stitch of clothing, NAKED. And he was walking right beside us. I was horrified. I tried to shield my daughter from the trauma of this. Where is hysterical blindness when you need it? Where is scouring powder when you want to score out your eyes because there are some things you can't un-see?

A moment of...WHAT WAS THAT? Followed by a moment of OH NO that couldn't be what we just saw! Followed by lots of moments of bent-over-double laughter. There we were in the middle of Frankfort, Germany, laughing so hard, so hysterically we couldn't even catch our breath.

Adam and Eve were naked in the garden, but when they sinned, it forever changed that whole dynamic. For us running around naked is not good, no matter how hot it is. I will have to say that nakedness offers a benefit besides being cooler...THERE IS NO LAUNDRY! But covering us up is the benefit of clothes and God saw that was necessary after sin entered. Someone should have explained that to the man who was out for a walk. (Not everyone gets social cues.)

Later, we did ask if somehow that was typical in Germany, you know naked people walking early in the morning. *"No,"* we were told, it was not.

Phew, that's a good thing, I may sometime want to go back.

Genesis 3

Adam and Eve sinned.

"Then the eyes of both of them were opened, and they realized they were naked; so they sewed fig leaves together and made coverings for themselves." Genesis 3:7

The Bible says their eyes were opened. Instantly they knew they were naked and needed a covering. Their solution? They sewed fig leaves together. It doesn't sound like the best idea. Leaves tend to shrink.

But don't we do the same thing? Oh it may not be fig leaves, we're too sophisticated for that, but have we ever sewn together pieces of the truth to create a covering? The words we say may be true, but we leave out some of the important facts so we cover our sin.

Then they heard a familiar sound. They hid. The Lord God had come to walk with them in the cool of the day. What a blissful thought, God coming to stroll with them in the evening, but they were hiding among the trees.

"But the Lord God called to the man, 'Where are you?'" Genesis 3:9

Such love. God already knew that they had sinned,

and yet He came. God already knew that they were hiding, and yet He spoke. His eyes never left them. His heart hadn't abandoned them. He came to them. God said, *"Where are you?"*

No matter what we've done.
No matter how far we've strayed.
No matter how much we try to hide, God still calls to us, *"Where are you?"*

The call is not because He doesn't know where we are, His eyes haven't left us. The call is so we will come to Him.

Day 27

We were invited for dinner. Our friends were absolutely sure that they were going to bless us with a special menu.

We were having whole lobsters for the very first time.

They had been flown in from the east coast for the evening. Dave stood in the kitchen watching as the wiggling crustaceans were admitted into the boiling water and he listened as each let out a distinct hiss. He knew it was a cry for help but he had no choice. He had to ignore the plea.

He tried not to consider that they looked like they had extended family that fell more into a category of critters that exterminators might visit. He just didn't care for the resemblance.

He watched as the pot was covered to allow them to steam. They went from brown to red. The pot was then uncovered and they were lifted onto warmed plates.

Eyes, tentacles, claws were all intact. Their body parts no longer functioned and yet it looked to him as if they still dared a stare. And thus their lifeless forms were carried by pallbearers to join the potatoes, corn, and salad.

Our host prayed and then we received the most disconcerting counsel of the night. *"Make sure you don't eat the green part. It's the lungs."*

The lungs?

It was at those words that Dave became lifeless and went from a healthy pink to a pasty white.

He whispered. *"I think I will just have a potato."*

The possibility of eating a lung knocked the air right out of him.

We had been promised a dinner of a lifetime. It had sounded good. At one point it even looked kind of good. But lung eating took away any possibility of an enjoyable dinner.

To Dave, what looked good on the outside, carried death on the inside.

Genesis 3

"But the Lord God called to the man,'Where are you?' He answered, 'I heard You in the garden, and I was afraid because I was naked; so I hid.'"
Genesis 2:9-10

This fruit that looked so good, the fruit that Satan promised would make them wise, and would make them like God, failed. For one taste of a piece of fruit, they now realized that they were naked, they were ashamed, they were afraid, and they were hiding from the One who created them, who loved them, who walked with them.

Sin does that. It looks inviting on the outside, but there is an incredibly high price for the fruit.

Day 28

"Mom, there is a major leak in my water bed."

Some words in our lives are so sweet they are worth remembering. Some are so moving you know you will never forget, and then there are those words that still the hands of time.

"A major leak in the water bed."

What do the words *"major leak"* mean in relationship to a waterbed? I was about to find out.

The water bed was a great invention for those who wanted to be rocked to sleep on the waves of the ocean or lulled to slumber by gentle movement. I don't think they are so popular any more. Ever wonder why?

I flew up the stairs to my eleven year old son's room. A leak? I'd say! There was a gaping wound in the center of the bed and water was bleeding out onto the floor. And to further complicate the matter, he had tried to solve the problem by simply placing cups around the four corners of the bed. A few cups placed strategically under the corners of the bed were not about to solve the dilemma. I held the two sides of the opening to try to stop the leaking water. Too late. I could hear the sound of water already dripping down to the first floor. I screamed for my son to grab a bucket from the garage. When he came in I grabbed a cup and started bailing while still trying to hold the two sides of the tear higher than the water level. I *'sweetly'* mentioned that it was good for him that my hands were otherwise engaged.

Water bed Thursday, the stuff of legends. I think it all began with a tiny puncture he had made in his bed. What would happen? Well a tiny leak happened which he covered with duct tape. But then curiosity got the better of him and he tore the tape back to see if the tiny leak was still there. Sure enough! And voila, it was waterbed Thursday. I called my sister-in-law for a shop vac. The work of drying out that floor, well, it was a mess. One tiny act led to a huge consequence.

I've been asked what his punishment was. I believe that sometimes the natural consequences are good punishments. The boy had no bed. He slept on the very hard floor for a very long time.

Genesis 3

In Genesis 3:11 it tell us that God spoke, *"Who told you that you were naked? Have you eaten from the tree that I commanded you not to eat from?"*

It wasn't that God didn't know, of course He knew. God knows everything we do. God knew Adam and Eve needed to confess their sin.

Adam answered, *"The woman You put here with me-she gave me some fruit from the tree, and I ate it."*

"Then the Lord God said to the woman, 'What is this you have done?'"

The woman said, 'The serpent deceived me and I ate.'" Genesis 3:12-13

The blame game, we do it too, our sin is someone else's fault. Even children know how to blame another child. It really comes pretty naturally. But the truth is they did it. They both ate the fruit. They both were guilty of the sin. And we are too. All of us have sinned.

We have all fallen short, but the good news is... the story isn't over.

Day 29

We mentioned worms and I agree; they are despicable, deplorable, disgusting little wriggling creatures. But their older, fatter, larger, more evil cousins are the ones who leave me running for higher ground when one even dares to enter my personal space.

Yes, I am talking about the 'S' word. Snakes. Snakes are the one brand of creature on the planet that I find no good use for at all. My words to live by when it comes to them, *"The only good snake is a dead one."*

But I guess no one told the snake clan living in the woods behind me that they might be heading for death row if they came into my yard. Because one audacious, gigantic black snake came to dwell under my front porch. Fortunately for me I usually use the garage entrance.

Now I can just hear some of you saying, *"But black snakes are good. They kill mice."* Here's the deal, I WOULD RATHER HAVE MICE! Please don't send out an invitation that mice are welcome at my house. I am not remotely saying that. It's just that given a choice between a mouse and a snake, I'll choose small furry creatures over slimy, slithery ones every time.

I guess looking back I saw signs that there was a snake under my porch. There seemed to be a winding trail in the mulch around my landscaping. There was dirt and debris next to the porch even after I swept it. But let me explain something. Sometimes when we don't want something to be true, we tell ourselves it isn't. We look at the evidence and say, *"No, that can't be right."* and move on with life.

It is also the way with sin. It slithers in a little at a time and we begin to tell ourselves, *"You know, it's not really that bad."* We close our eyes to the evil lurking, crouching at the door, waiting for the door to open a crack so it can wriggle all the way in.

My kids came to visit. My son-in-law saw this limbless, scaly reptile poke its pointy little head out from under the porch looking to see who had dared to step onto its cement roof.

Ryan whispered to my daughter, *"Don't tell your mom but there's a snake under the porch. I'll take care of it."*

Too late! I had opened the door enough to hear part... *"Whaaaaaaat is under my front porch?"*

Heroes! We see them in the movies but we also see them in everyday life. They come at just the right time, swoop in and annihilate, crush, exterminate to rid the world of villains and vipers.

I didn't ask how he coaxed the thing out into open air and I didn't see the actual duel to the death but my son-in-law came back into my house.

The score: son-in-law 1, snake 0.

Later my brother-in-law filled the vacant apartment under the porch with spray foam insulation. I wanted to make sure that there wasn't a vacancy any longer.

I wanted to make absolutely sure the evil couldn't get in.

So what can we do to insulate us against the evil lurking in the shadows or just under the porch? Know the Word of God and pray. These are the weapons. Ephesians 6:10-18 gives us that directive.

Genesis 3

Genesis 3:15 *"And I will put enmity between you and the woman..."*

That means hatred. It's Biblical...enough said.

Day 30

I bought a coffee mug. Oh, not just any mug, this one is a hand crafted, specially designed, piece of art. It drips with glaze the color of the mountains and is shaped just right to fit into the space in my car, a most useful piece of art.

It's amazing how the artist does it. He slaps a lump of clay, common dirt, onto his potter's wheel and begins to spin the wheel. The clay rises in his hands. It's fun to watch. A shape emerges, then a design as he weaves his hands in and out, applying pressure and touch. He knows exactly how to do it, but sometimes the piece gets a little marred. No worries, the potter just picks up the clay, slaps it back down and begins again until exactly the right shape forms. He carefully works until he knows it is just right. Then he removes it from the flywheel.

However, the process for this useful work of art has just begun. Next it dries. Oh not too fast, it could crack, just the right amount of dryness. The cup simply must age, cure, for a little while to become useable.

Then when the curing process is complete, it's time for the kiln-1500 degrees. That's really hot. I don't usually cook at such high temperatures unless dinner has to be ready in one minute and we want a significant char on the food.

But into the fire this piece must go. After a scorching eight hours and cooling overnight, the cup is removed so it can be glazed. Beautiful color is poured into the piece, covering it completely on the inside. That done; it's dipped into another glaze to add dimension. Then more color from glaze that is allowed to drip down the sides, until the colors of the snow-capped mountain peaks, or the crimson sunset, or the green leafy forest emerge. Another firing, this time 2400 degrees merges glaze to clay forever. The melted glaze oozes into the porous clay and the two become one, never to be separated again.

I like this new cup so much that I wanted to share. I bought its twin, not identical, no two are ever exactly the same, but very similar, as a Christmas gift.

While some of the artisan's pieces are more exotic, more intricate, more expensive, this one is perfect for me. Some pieces are useful only on special occasions, or only as decorative pieces. My cup is useful everyday as I sit down to read and study God's Word, or jump in the car, coffee in hand. Every day as I pick it up, I'm grateful I own it. I'm grateful that a glob of clay can be made into something not just useful, but beautiful.

Shhhh, Kath bought a similar cup and left it at my house. Maybe she won't notice and then I can have two. Oh wait, she just called.

Genesis 3

God took a piece of clay, common dirt, and formed it beautifully in His hands. Man was indeed perfect, no flaw. God also fashioned the woman, again no flaws.

But then... they sinned. Now they were marred, misshapen, bent a new direction. Satan in the guise of the serpent had enticed; Satan had won a victory.

It seemed all was lost. But right there in the middle of the sin was God's provision, the promise of a Savior, born from the seed of a woman. There could be a way back.

God spoke to the serpent, *"And I will put enmity between you and the woman, and between your offspring and hers; He will crush your head, and you will strike His heel."* Genesis 3:15

The incredible promise of One who could be victorious over the evil that had just entered the world.

But you see I am also that lump of clay. The Master Potter put me on that flywheel and molded and crafted me. Then I was marred, not by His hands, but by my choosing. Yet, He graciously reshaped me into something useful. He poured

His Holy Spirit into and over me and there have been times in the fire. We have become one, and He isn't leaving.

I have His Word on it. The world left its mark, but He is burning away the impurities, and can even turn those ugly past scars into works of art. I may not be the most decorative, but I can be useful. I'm good with the Lord picking me up every day, just a piece of clay, shaped, molded, glazed, fired and filled with His coffee...make that living water.

Today why not look at Jeremiah 18 while you have your coffee.

Day 31

My husband was ill, not just a little, but a lot.
He came home from a trip not feeling well. After a few
days he went to see the doctor. They thought it was a
muscle. Some medication, and just in case, a trip to
the specialist was ordered. The specialist also said that
it was just a muscle, he would be better in a few days.
Those days came and went, but the problem did not.

We called for another appointment. This time it was
a different medication, some rest and the assurance
that he would be better shortly. But he was not better
shortly. No! Instead of better, he got worse. The pain
was now constant and severe. He could no longer
eat. My strong capable husband could no longer get
out of bed without my help. In a few short, well, they
seemed incredibly long, weeks, he lost thirty pounds.
I took him back to the specialist. This time he was so
ill he could no longer sit in the waiting room. He lay
on the floor, eyes closed, barely moving.

Here's a tip. If you don't want to wait in the doctor's
office, play dead, they take you right away.

The nurse walked in, saw John and called his name
first. This time the doc said *"Surgery, immediately!
Go next door to the hospital."* We slowly walked, my
husband leaning on me, every step now an effort.

We were supposed to go in the front and fill out the paper work. I somehow missed that part. Besides the back door was closer. We walked in the back. As soon as John saw a gurney, he flopped onto it. The nurses took one look and decided they could do the paper work from his bedside.

And then... surgery. He was so grateful to be relieved from the constant pain. The surgical pain felt like blessed relief. He was better, on the road to recovery. He had had an infection that was causing all his suffering and pain. Now gone, he started to feel better.

But infection is like sin, it crouches, waiting, and can come back, and sometimes with a vengeance.

The *"better"* lasted only a few days and his pain, and weakness, and not eating, returned.

More doctors, more surgery, more medication, and then finally... finally... health.

Genesis 3, 2 Corinthians

"I can do this. I'm not hurting anyone else." Those words spoken silently, or even out loud to others, justify sin. Perhaps you've heard them, perhaps you've spoken them.

"As long as it's just me, as long as my actions just involve me and don't hurt anyone else..." But it's just not true.

When Eve ate the fruit, when Adam took the first bite, the result was enormous. The result of one act of disobedience was global and eternal. Sin entered the world, pain and suffering came too.

"To the woman He said, 'I will make your pains in childbearing very severe; with painful labor you will give birth to children. Your desire will be for your husband, and he will rule over you.'" Genesis 3:16

Yes, this is about child birth and anyone who has given birth, or watched a woman giving birth, or heard a woman giving birth, knows that there is pain. This is the kind of pain that is indescribable pain. It can put a woman in the valley of the shadow of death. But this is not the only pain in our world. Once this door opened, once pain entered, it was not limited to just labor and delivery. We are all marked with its stain. Tiny babies cry from tiny tummy aches and ear infections. Toddlers whimper over knee scrapes and sore throats. And then there's cancer and migraines and leprosy and ebola, and burning, stinging, aching, throbbing, constant, awful pain from a million different ailments, and diseases, and wounds, and man hurting man, and meanness, and awfulness in our world. From the tops of our heads to the souls of our feet we can and do feel pain. Sometimes it's just nagging pain, sometimes it's throwing up, barely able to draw a breath, severe, agonizing, horrific pain.

Pain and suffering came into the world with a vengeance because of one sin. But how much pain and suffering are in the world because of our sin? How much pain and suffering are in the world because of all sin?

Jesus never sinned, but He bore the pain of it any way. He was struck, hit, whipped, beaten, tormented, spit on, beard pulled out, mocked, tortured, nailed to a wooden cross.

Excruciating was a word coined to describe the agony of the cross. This wasn't for His sin, He had none. This was to pay for and buy back not just that one sin, but all sin, not just Adam and Eve's sin, but yours and mine. And He did it.

So here's the age old question, *"Why is there still pain and suffering in the world, if Jesus died to pay the price for it, why is it still here?"*

Here's the answer. I don't know. But this I do know, God can still use it. Our stories of pain, suffering, even loss can merge with His to become testimonies of God's sweet faithfulness. Yes, there is still pain in our world. Yes, there is still suffering. Once in, it stayed. But pain and suffering are not the victor; Jesus is. He rose. He conquered. And even when we walk through that valley of death, even when the pain is excruciating, He promises His presence.

And can I let you in on some very good news? There is coming a time and place when all pain, all suffering, all those agonizing moments will be placed under the feet of the Savior and crushed and discarded never to be seen or felt again.

"Therefore we do not lose heart. Though outwardly we are wasting away, yet inwardly we are being renewed day by day. For our light and momentary troubles are achieving for us an eternal glory that far outweighs them all. So we fix our eyes not on what is seen, but on what is unseen, since what is seen is only temporary, but what is unseen is eternal." 2 Corinthians 4:16-18.

Day 32

Most people don't have many memories of events before the age of three. But I have a whopper.

My mom had an industrial styled iron. There are some appliances you just have to have when you have as many kids as she had. This was before the days of permanent press. Please don't look up the time frame when that came on the market. We have already confessed to being old, so let's leave it at that.

Mom would sit down in front of it, take the wrinkled clothes, place them under a roller and watch as it pressed them. It was nothing short of magical. I really wanted to understand how you could take something that looked so old and wrinkled and make it come out so perfect.

Well, okay, I was only three and so I am pretty certain that I didn't really process all of my wonder in exactly that way, but I do remember being extremely curious about the thing.

Mom had one rule: STAY AWAY FROM IT! Good rule, wouldn't you say? She thought so and if I knew then what I know now I would have agreed. But I didn't.

I remember as if it happened moments ago. My sisters came up on Mom's right side as she was pressing some sheets. She turned to motion for them to step back and I saw my chance. I reached in the basket of clothes, picked up a sock, ran up to her other side and slipped it under the roller.

Here was the problem: I had no idea how it worked. I didn't realize that the roller had to be stopped before you put anything in, then you let go and it did the work.

But the roller was not stopped and I didn't let go. Before Mom even grasped what was happening, my left hand was being sucked into the hot roller and pressed lifeless.

I want to make this perfectly clear. I did this on purpose. I picked up the sock and put it under that roller knowing that I was not allowed to touch it.

She stopped it in seconds that felt like hours and lifted my hand from the blistering heat.

She got me to the hospital as soon as possible only to discover that I had third degree burns.

It took five surgeries to get my hand to the place where I could carry a glass of water across the kitchen.

It is fascinating how my little hand that looked so new could come out of that thing looking so old and wrinkled.

But it did. I was left with terrible, ugly scars and thanks to the taunting from the kids I went to school with, I was also left with the knowledge that it wasn't just my hand that was ugly.

Everything about me was ugly.

For years I dealt with that belief and, okay, on this one, maybe I did need therapy, but I have to tell you that I think I can meet the best Therapist in the pages of His Word.

And that is exactly where I met mine.

I am going to reiterate. I did this. It was direct disobedience and the consequences were real and they were permanent.

But my disobedience met His obedience.

Let me share a couple of life-changing verses about scars. Isaiah 49:15-16 says *"Can a mother forget the baby at her breast and have no compassion on the child she has borne? Though she may forget, I will not forget you! See, I have engraved you on the palms of my hands; your walls are ever before me."*

Did you see those beautiful words? I have been

engraved on the palms of His hands. When did that happen?

I believe it happened at the cross.

As those nails went in, my name went on. My sin put Him there. His love kept Him there.

Do you know what I hear His heart whispering to mine? *"Kris, it is finished. Those scars are no longer yours. They are mine."*

Are the scars on my hand ugly? You might think so but I don't any longer. I now see beauty.

His scars are real and they are permanent. But every time He looks at them, He sees my face. Now, every time I look at mine, I see His.

"...I will not forget you. See, I have engraved you on the palms of my hands..."

Genesis 3, Isaiah 52, 53

It was one sin, one single sin. It was a piece of fruit, taken from the wrong tree in the Garden. Adam and Eve ate the wrong thing. How often have we eaten the wrong thing, or done the wrong thing, or said the wrong thing? So I guess we can identify.

But this one sin had enormous results.

First, Adam and Eve were separated from the very presence of God.

Next, they knew that they were naked. The light of God's glory no longer clothed them.

Then came the consequence of pain and suffering, not just for them, but for all people, for all time.

Then, thorns, thistles, toil, labor, hard work, the ground was cursed, the world fell under the curse.

Sin came into the world. What began with a piece of fruit, grew into hate, murder, abuse, rape, every awful, terrible sin. Sin has not stood still. It has grown and multiplied like cancer cells. It is rampant.

And then, death. Satan's words, *"You will not surely die,"* have proven to be a lie every single time we attend a funeral.

God's Words in Genesis 2:16b-17, "...*You are free to eat from any tree in the garden; but you must not eat from the tree of the knowledge of good and evil, for when you eat of it you will surely die.*" And sure enough God's Word has proven true over and over. Death entered the world.

It was one sin, one single sin and then came the promise.

The seed, the offspring of the woman would someday crush the head of the serpent, Satan.

Then in another garden the miracle unfolded.

The Bible tells us in Isaiah 53:6, "*We all, like sheep, have gone astray, each of us has turned to our own way; and the Lord has laid on Him the iniquity of us all.*"

God laid on Jesus the sin of the world. This was Adam and Eve's sin but this was also the sin of the world. Every sin, from every person, for all time was placed on the sinless Savior.

Jesus began to sweat great drops of His own blood as he toiled and labored against the sin.

He was stripped naked and beaten so severely that He was no longer recognizable as a man. Isaiah 52:14 "*Just as there were many who were appalled at Him, His appearance was so disfigured beyond that of any human being and His form marred beyond human likeness..."*

He then endured flogging, pain, humiliation, and nakedness. He wore thorns as a crown and was nailed to a tree.

He experienced the separation of sin, not His own sin, He had none, but the separation from God because of all sin. Matthew 27:46 says, *"About three in the afternoon Jesus cried out in a loud voice, 'Eli, Eli, lema sabachthani?' (which means, 'My God, my God, why have you forsaken me?')"*

The result of sin was separation from God, nakedness, shame, pain, sweat, thorns, agony and then death.

Sin came into the world because of one man's sin. The price was the death of God for all man's sin.

Jesus, God With Us, died for the sin of the world.

Most of us miss some social cues. Rare is the person who has been trained in any and all situations as to what is appropriate in society. Those who have that kind of education are usually called royalty.

But most of us also pick up enough to get us through life without too many blunders. But, again, there are gaps.

One of the girls on my dorm floor had a big gap. She would forget to put clothes on when she went to open the door to her dorm room. It only took most of us one visit to her room to figure out that it would be better to chat with her in the cafeteria. Now I will edit this a little. She was naked but she always had her purse.

I am the first to admit that I love purses but I usually leave mine in the closet when I head to the shower. But again we all look at the world from a different set of social norms. May I say, though, that purses don't cover up nakedness any better than leaves.

As hard as they tried, Adam and Eve knew that the leaves were not sufficient as a covering. They did not want to stand before God in their nakedness. So they hid. The problem is that you can never completely hide your sin. There are always at least two who know. You know and so does The Lord.

From the very moment of their disobedience they knew they needed to be covered. And so God covered them. An innocent animal was slain to cover them up.

We have needed our sin to be covered ever since. But in reality, not just covered but done away with.

Genesis 3

Fig leaves, Adam and Eve's attempt to cover their sinfulness. Leaves shrink, so not the best covering. But it wasn't just Adam and Eve. Throughout history mankind has made attempts to cover his own sin. Being good enough, or giving enough, or giving up enough, or doing enough, or trying hard enough, or even being religious enough, but none of it is enough because nothing we can do can wash away our sin. It has always been that God must cover us.

'The Lord God made garments of skin for Adam and his wife and clothed them.' Genesis 3:21

God used the death of that animal to make a covering for them. From that moment on the sacrificial system was in place, the shedding of the blood of an animal to cover the sin. God saw the blood and an atonement, a covering, was made. But the death of a lamb or a bull or a goat never washed away a person's sin, it only covered it.

It's like when we use a credit card. We are not yet really paying. We are simply making a covering for the debt. The payment isn't actually made until the money leaves the account.

For 4000 years the sacrifices were God's continued promise that the payment for sin was coming. Every one of those sacrifices pointed forward to the real payment, the death of The Lamb of God. It was only when He died that the payment was made. He cried out, *"It is finished!"*

Or as it can also be translated, *"Paid in full!"*

Day 34

Sometimes in life we get flattened. Situations roll over us with a giant steamroller and crush us under the weight. I was flattened. My head hung so far down people couldn't see my eyes. In fact I wore my hair so that it covered part of my face. I was trying to be invisible. I didn't want anyone to read the pain.

At that time I was attending a rather large church. It was a good place for me to blend into the shadows. I could sit in a place where I could easily get out a back door if the pain was too much. Sometimes the pain was too much.

The New Year was approaching. I was praying for a new beginning. The pastor began to talk about things you could do if you needed a miracle in the new year. I did, so I listened. He mentioned fasting.

Now let me interject here for a moment. Fasting is not one of those disciplines that gets lots of attention. It's not a fun thing to do. It means giving up food. I like food. I like feeling full. I don't like feeling hungry.

But the more I listened the more compelling it became. I wanted and needed God to move in my situation. I needed His hand to lead me. The words of the pastor drove me to study the verses he had mentioned.

Isaiah 58:6-9 began my study. The benefits of fasting were right there. Fasting helps to loose the chains of injustice, untie the cords of the yoke, set the oppressed free and break every yoke.

I also read Matthew 4:1-11. Jesus fasted for forty days. Here He was, God incarnate and He needed to fast. He needed to break the earthly ties with food for a while and have perfect communion with the Father. As I studied, it became apparent to me that if Jesus fasted, how much more did I need to break earthly ties with food to pray and seek Him in a desperate time.

Then of course there were some physical benefits like the obvious weight loss. But there is also allowing the body to rest and the release of toxins.

I was in. Corporate fasting has some benefits as well since this pastor was calling the whole church to join. People are praying for you and with you. You get encouragement from others. There is accountability when you are tempted to stop.

The fast was for 21+ days depending on your size and medical situation.

Was it easy to go without food? No. Was it easy for Jesus? No. After the forty days he would have been at the point of literal starvation. When you are starving you will eat almost anything. When Satan came and told him to turn the stones into bread, that would have been an unbelievable temptation. His body, every cell would have been crying out for food. Yet, Jesus stood against the enemy meeting every challenge. He was and is the victor.

At the end of the fast God did do some wonderful things. I was in a small group and I was reflecting on the way I had been praying. You see through this I had prayed for God to move on behalf of someone who was oppressed. I wanted God to release him from the clutches of Satan. I had prayed and prayed that God would set him free. Did that answer come right after the fast?

No, it did not.

I said this to my small group, *"But I prayed that God would set the oppressed free."* You see I wanted that answer right away. I wanted the person I was praying for to be changed. But he didn't want to be changed, at least not right then, and God allows people to make their own choices even if they hurt themselves or others.

One of the women in the group had been staring at me, studying my face. She had noticed something and she said, *"But Kathie, you are free."* When she said it I had to kind of catch my breath. You see she had been looking at my countenance, because my head was no longer hanging down, my hair was no longer covering my eyes. People could see that God was releasing me. I had been flattened, but God was lifting my head. Through the experience He had drawn me close to His heart and He was healing my broken heart. Yes, others could see the change. I began to see it too.

Genesis 3, Matthew 4

When Adam and Eve ate the fruit, it wasn't because they were hungry. The garden was lush with vegetation, abounding in every kind of fruit imaginable. They sinned because they wanted the fruit. They wanted what was forbidden. They wanted what looked good. They wanted what would make them wise. They wanted to be like God. They could have picked any of the hundreds of fruits, including the fruit from the tree of life, because it was also right there, but they didn't. They could have chosen to eat from what would give them eternal life, but they didn't.

But the story doesn't end there.

Jesus went into the desert. It wasn't lush, it wasn't green. It was the barren dry desert, and there He fasted for forty days.

He was hungry. He was starving!

"The tempter came to him and said, 'If You are the Son of God, tell these stones to become bread.'

Jesus answered, 'it is written: 'Man shall not live on bread alone, but on every word that comes from the mouth of God.'" Matthew 4:3-4

Adam and Eve said *"Yes"* to the temptation but walked away from the tree of life. Jesus said *"No"* to the temptation but walked toward the cross, the tree of life for us.

Day 35

It is about 3:00 in the morning. I've been awake since 2:00. My sisters and I are trying to finish this second devotional.

I've been working on a story about warts...if that won't keep you glued to this book, I don't know what will. I know the world is just waiting for a good story about warts. So take a deep breath and be patient. It is probably coming soon.

But I just got interrupted.

Let me preface that with a reminder. I am the one with the brain tumor. When I found out, I swallowed pretty hard.

At that same time, we had to say good-bye to our faithful little dog named Sarah. We had adopted her when our kids were little. When we got her, she already had a name. Her name was Whiskey. We decided to change it, because a pastor standing outside calling for whiskey might not be the best way to impact our neighborhood.

But we had to put her to sleep. Dave bought her a Happy Meal® (She should have known something was up.) and took her to the vet. He cried. I cried.

But the days ahead for her were going to be degenerative and pain-filled.

There were other things going on in our lives that easily could have been tipping points to a crash, but they weren't.

But there was something that did tip the balance for me. It was something I noticed as I was getting ready to step into the garage.

It was about two inches long and running along the baseboard of our hallway. I collapsed. When I got to school, I put my head down and wept. It was IN MY HOUSE!

I called Dave. I didn't ask. I wasn't polite. I demanded! *"Go anywhere you have to. Get as many traps as you can find! Buy all the poison in the world."*

I didn't care about animal rights or protecting the environment or even sounding sane. Mice leave evidence that they have been there. (We talked about that in our last book.) But what I failed to mention is that they mark their territory...every place they put their filthy claws.

Can you tell that there aren't words big enough in my vocabulary to describe my disgust?

I wanted it out and I wanted it out now!

Why am I bringing this up? I have little bags of chips on my table and I just heard one crackle.

If that wasn't a small tremor shaking the house, and I see one of those creatures, I will not be able to finish my wart story. I don't want to disappoint you but I will have to go get the house ready.

WE'RE MOVING!

Genesis 3, John 14

Genesis 3:22-24, *"And the Lord God said, 'The man has now become like one of us, knowing good and evil. He must not be allowed to reach out his hand and take also from the tree of life and eat and live forever.' So the Lord God banished him from the Garden of Eden to work the ground from which he had been taken. After He drove the man out, He placed on the east side of the Garden of Eden cherubim and a flaming sword, flashing back and forth to guard the way to the tree of life."*

The price of sin:
Adam and Eve thought the fruit would add to their life, it didn't. Instead it robbed them. Sin took them from God's presence. It robbed them of their innocence, their purity. It took them from the Garden. It took them into the world. Then God lovingly blocked the way to the tree of life. God didn't want them to eat from that tree and live forever in that state. He blocked the way so He could make a Way back into His Presence, back to purity and cleanness and a relationship with Him.

Jesus answered, *"I am the way and the truth and the life. No one comes to the Father except through me."* John 14:6.

What sin stole, Jesus restored.

Warts. Nasty word. Nastier yet is the look of the things. You usually notice when you have one or two and take care of it with an over-the-counter freeze thing or bottle of some solution and in a few days you are good to go.

Now I'm pretty sure you don't want a lesson on warts. That discussion probably ranks a little below a chart on the different types of squash you can purchase like butternut, cushaw, acorn. See, isn't that fascinating? And you thought I wasn't much of a cook.

But warts? There should be a chart. There are several different kinds and I didn't know that. I somehow got a couple of some rare kind on my ankle and didn't even notice...until I had used enough new razors to spread them. It looked like poison ivy and itched like poison ivy.

I went to the doctor.

All he could say when I pointed out my *"poison ivy"* was *"Oh, my!"*

"Oh, my!" What did that mean?

He explained. I had managed to spread the things all over my legs. Okay, okay. As much as I hate taking medicine, what kind would he prescribe?

Nope. The answer was not medicine. The answer was burning. Yes, burning each one off my legs. Now he could numb each place, which meant a shot and then the burning or just the burning. He had to do both.

I believe he invented the Taser after this.

I couldn't catch my breath until it was all over. It took several visits and counseling after...no, not really...but it is not something I ever want to do again. I had over a hundred places, or maybe it was a million, I don't remember exactly. They were dark days.

I have scars on my legs and shorter teeth from clenching them so tightly. But it is an object lesson to me of how quickly the dark side can take over my life if I let even little things go unnoticed.

There are different kinds of warts. The worst kind is named sin and it can move pretty fast.

Genesis 3, Isaiah 1

They left the abundance. From now on the crops wouldn't just grow; Adam and Eve would need to plant. However, the weeds and the thorns and the thistles would grow, so they couldn't simply tend the garden; they would need to work it. Toil, labor, sweat, work, how often did they crawl into bed at night, so tired from their labor, and think about life in the Garden? How often did they remember that they had been clothed in the Light of God's Presence and looked down at the animal skins they were wearing, now soiled by the dirt and sweat?

"The Lord God made garments of skin for Adam and his wife and clothed them." Genesis 1:21

God had taken the life of an animal to clothe Adam and Eve. Their nakedness was covered. But this was nothing like being wrapped in God's glory.

How often did they ask themselves, why had they listened to the serpent?

How often do we?

We can, like Adam and Eve, look back and remember choices we made, sins we committed and our lives took a turn. We wish we hadn't, but we did.

But God's promise, even though it had not yet
been written down, was for Adam and Eve. The
promise, even though it is now centuries old, is for
us..."*Though your sins are like scarlet, they will
be as white as snow*". Isaiah 1:18

A promise greater than the greatest sin.

Day 37

It was one of those phone calls you never want to receive.

It had already been a long Saturday. I had been out of town for the day and once home was ready to call it a day when the phone rang.

The voice on the other end said, *"You need to go to the hospital immediately. Lindy has fallen from the catwalk at church and the ambulance is on its way."*

Over the phone I could hear the sirens. I knew help was on the way for our daughter. But John and I knew virtually nothing of her condition, how badly she was hurt, only that she had fallen from the catwalk, a considerable distance, over thirty feet. How had this happened? But no time for questions, just move.

We hurried to change and go. In the car I remember praying, *"Lord, I don't know what this means for Lindy or for us, but at this very moment, I choose to trust You."*

John dropped me at the door of the hospital. He parked the car. I raced to the reception desk. *"Lindy Kizlin? She fell and was brought here."*

They checked, *"No, no such patient."*

My husband and I had been at least twenty or twenty–five minutes dressing and getting to the hospital. I had heard the ambulance. This was the right hospital; it was only a minute or two from the church.

My thoughts raced, *"Why wasn't she here?"*

And then a worse thought, *"They didn't bring her because she died; they were taking my child to the morgue."*

I fought not to lose it. Tears of grief were already flooding my eyes. Perhaps God had called our girl home. I wasn't sure I could bear it. Would I really trust Him? I sat down to wait.

And then, Lindy's friend came racing in, *"She's in the ambulance and she's talking."*

Tears... tears...blessed tears of relief, not grief.

Lindy lay in the hospital for several days, a fractured skull, so sick she couldn't lift her head. Every single doctor who came into her room wanted to hear, *"Now, how did this happen?"*

Neurologists, neurosurgeons, they see a lot of head trauma, kids riding bikes without helmets, people in car accidents or motorcycle collisions, they see a lot. But I think Lindy was a first.

One neurologist came into her room, sat down, leaned back in the chair, crossed his legs and began, *"I've heard a little about this, but now explain exactly how this happened."*

He waited for the story, by this time I had pieced it together from the friends who were with Lindy...if I had known she was going to do this foolhardy...well that's another story.

It was supposed to be a special day at church. The theme was *"Gear Up for Ministry"*. Catchy title and various ministries would enter the sanctuary in various ways, riding a bike, on a scooter, even a motorcycle was mentioned. A few of the youth ministry leaders, and Lindy was one, decided to repel into the sanctuary from the catwalk.

Yes, you heard me, REPEL. But they had better practice first. The first run through went fine, but just to be safe (Did you catch that, *"just to be SAFE?"*) a second practice. Lindy had long hair, and NO HELMET. What was she thinking? Her hair caught in the rope and when she reached up to free it, she let go of the rope. On the way down she realized that she had just made a very bad choice. Lindy fell somewhere close to fifteen feet onto the wooden platform.

The doctor's response, *"I'm guessing this is not a*

Presbyterian church." I'm thinking he had never seen this happen at his Sunday morning service.

His second response was to explain what neurologists called D-ten. It meant dead at ten feet. He said that fifty percent of people falling over ten feet don't survive the fall. He recommended she not do it again.

Ummm YEAH! I completely agreed.

Lindy came home from the hospital not quite as good as new. Rest, quiet. But then on the third day after the fall, a new complication, her face felt strange, a little numb, she couldn't quite move one side of her mouth.

I called the doctor. His words, *"Meet me in the emergency room!"*

Swelling was causing the nerves to her face to be pinched. Half of Lindy's beautiful face was drooping. Half of her lovely smile was a frown. Paralysis.

"Was this permanent?" We wanted to know.

The doctor could not answer. He simply didn't know. *"Go home, rest, wait and see."* Our beautiful girl was just a little bit broken.

And then, several days later, another phone call. This time it was from a young man at our church named Chris. He spoke, *"Could I take you and John to breakfast?"*

"Of course."

At breakfast he asked for our permission to date our daughter, the one whose face now drooped, the daughter who now dribbled water out of her not working mouth, the one who wasn't yet quite as good as new.

Chris didn't wait to see if she would recover fully. He hadn't waited to see if her face would return to its perfect state. (I can say she's perfect, I'm the Mom.) Chris came for her in her broken state. We had already observed that Chris liked Lindy, but this was a magnificent picture of love. This was a convincing proof that he qualified as a worthy suitor.

Our answer? *"Yes!"* We did caution that she also would need to say *"Yes."*

Lindy carries a few remains of the fall, neck pain, a little hearing loss, but on her wedding day, both sides of her mouth could form her lovely smile. The paralysis in her face slowly went away.

Ten years, two beautiful little girls later, Chris says she fell for him.

I say such great love drew her to him.

Genesis 3, Romans 5

Adam and Eve fell. The choice they made caused brokenness, hurt, pain; life would never be the same. The world would never be the same.

A call reached out across the universe. Was there anyone who could buy back the brokenness? Was there anyone who was worthy to redeem?

The answer:
"You see, at just the right time, when we were still powerless, Christ died for the ungodly. Very rarely will anyone die for a righteous person, though for a good person someone might possibly dare to die. But God demonstrates His own love for us in this: While we were still sinners, Christ died for us." Romans 5:6-8

Did you know that He wants to become your bridegroom? Did you know that He is more than willing to take you in your broken state? Are you aware that He wants to return to you a lovely smile and clothe you in white? Did you know that you can breathe in all His loveliness and exhale all the junk and stuff you have carried for so long? Do you know why?

Because on a cross He uttered three words and breathed His last breath, *"It is finished!"*

The price for sin paid. From Adam to us, the debt bought back.

Day 38

I teach kindergarten. It means that as soon as my students walk into the classroom my life is a flurry of activity. But one of my goals is to teach them how to work quietly at their tables for short periods of time, while I test students or read in small groups or get things ready for our next activity.

It was during one of those quiet times one day that I heard a gasp from one of my students. I looked up and stared straight into the face of an enormous black crow. He looked as if he could be in a heavyweight competition and emerge without a scratch. Even though he was out of his natural habitat and now in mine, he looked way more comfortable than I felt.

But I had to wonder how long it was going to stay that way. What was racing through my mind was the picture of my twenty little five-year-olds being dive-bombed by this behemoth and the utter terror, hysteria, and emotional scars this encounter was about to leave. (And that was just me.)

I didn't know how my students would come out. But what I did know was that my only goal was to get them out of there and into a safe place.

I started to whisper, *"Boys and girls. We have a guest in our room and we don't want to scare him. Would you please get up and tip-toe out of the room with me?"*

And do you know what? They did. They didn't make one sound. That crow just cocked his head and watched as we quietly surrendered our territory to him. You could almost hear him smirking. *"Yep, won this round without a shot fired!"*

My students followed me down the hall as I made my way to the maintenance department. As soon as I found one of the guys, he could tell that something was very wrong. I simply mouthed the words but he could hear their shout. *"THERE IS A CROW IN MY ROOM!"*

And in a few minutes the problem was taken care of and we were back in our room. I have no idea how they got the thing out, but they did.

I may have whispered, *"Nevermore."*

Genesis 3

"Nevermore"

Nevermore is a very final statement. It speaks to the fact that the door is closed. For Adam and Eve the door closed forever. They would never be able to enter that garden again. Yes, it was a result of their sin. It was one of the consequences of their choice. They had to leave that beautiful place.

But it was even more than that. It came out of God's heart of love. Everything that He does comes out of a heart of love. He would not allow them to be able to go back to eat from the tree of life and live forever apart from Him.

"So the Lord God banished him from the Garden of Eden to work the ground from which he had been taken." Genesis 3:23

Day 39

Have you noticed, that with each new family addition, laundry grows exponentially? My three children were little. It seemed like all I did was pick up dirty socks, dingy shirts, and grimy pants. I made so many trips back and forth down the hallway from the bedrooms to the laundry room I couldn't begin to count them in a week.

Maybe you can identify. It's a job that's never done but always needs doing. One afternoon I had just gathered up clothes from my little girls' rooms. I was headed to the laundry room with my arms loaded. It would be a relief to put the dirty clothes down in the baskets. I made it about halfway there. For no *"apparent"* reason I stopped. I was in the kitchen-dining area.

But suddenly (Suddenlies are those moments that happen when we least expect them.) I felt absolutely compelled to drop the laundry. Now, this wasn't at all like me. I like things neat and tidy so dropping a load of dirty clothes was completely out of my character. But it seemed urgent. So I dropped the clothes right in the middle of the floor. I actually felt like I was being pulled. I HAD to go into the living room to check on the kids. I just absolutely had to. So I did.

My daughters were there watching TV. But the two year old was coughing and making a wheezing sound. I took one look at her and knew something was wrong. I instantly reacted, grabbed and turned her over. She was gagging. Finally she coughed up something and spit it out. It was a metal screw about two inches long. I don't know where it came from, but I saw where it had been. It had been in her throat and she had been choking on it.

Was it an angel that caused me to feel so compelled to throw down an armload of dirty clothes to check on the kids?

Angels have big jobs. The Bible talks about angel visits.

Could it have been an angel who stood at my head when I was having surgery?

I had been told to check with the anesthesiologist to see if he was going to be with me the whole time. His native language was not English so his speech was broken, but I understood the word, *"No"*

That made me nervous. What if something happened like my blood pressure dropping because I was in too deep a sleep? What if I woke up and they weren't finished? I didn't like any of those possibilities.

But when I arrived in the operating room a man

stood behind me. I had no idea who he was because I couldn't see him, but I could hear him talking. He had just returned from a mission trip.

Missions?

I like missions, I listened. I could only hear his voice. He was speaking perfect English as he described his trip. Then he started to hum a song. I continued to listen.

I finally asked him, *"What are you humming?"*

He laughed, *"Do you recognize the song?"*

I did. *"Is it All Night, All Day, Angels Watching Over Me, O Lord?"*

"Yes," he said, *"Oh, and I'm your anesthesiologist. I'm going to be here with you the ENTIRE time."*

What happened to the other doctor who said he would leave after the anesthetic was started? Who was this? I went to sleep with the assurance that God was watching and maybe, just maybe had sent an angel to stand behind my head.

Angels have big jobs to do. The Bible talks about angel visits.

Then there was my sister, who was driving her

daughter to kindergarten on a busy Cincinnati highway. She looked into her side mirror. All clear. She turned her car to the left to pull into the passing lane. The car wouldn't move.

She said, *"It was as if a giant hand held my car, I could not turn it."*

Just as quickly another car whizzed past her. This driver would have plowed right into her side of the car. Had the Lord sent an angel to keep my sister's car in place?

Angels have big jobs to do. The Bible talks about angel visits.

Some years ago I heard a man talking about Cherubim. He described them as little baby angels who fly around the throne of God. I completely disagreed. That is not how the Bible describes them. Angels are not little babies with wings. They are big and mighty and powerful.

God sends them to do BIG jobs. I believe He is still sending them.

Genesis 3, Hebrews 13

In Genesis we see cherubim with a flashing sword sent to guard the entrance to the garden. The scripture tells us in 3:24 *"After He drove the man out, He placed on the East side of the Garden of Eden cherubim and a flaming sword flashing back and forth to guard the way to the tree of life."*

For close to 6,000 years this entrance has been guarded by an angel wielding a flashing sword. People have longed to find the tree of life. Some have given their lives searching for it. God sent an angel to guard it and to date, it has never been found. And until God is ready for the tree of life to be revealed, it never will be found.

Angels are messengers. They do what God tells them to do. Sometimes they strike fear, but they also bring good news, protect and maybe, they just show up suddenly.

Hebrews 13:2 says, *"Do not forget to show hospitality to strangers, for by so doing some people have shown hospitality to angels without knowing it."*

Day 40

Death lived under my house.

My husband is a pastor and for a long time he kept a casket in the crawl space. Yes, he does funerals and no, he wasn't saving it for someone more needy than us.

I don't think all pastors have caskets stored under their homes. I think he saw it in the funeral home window and just had to have it.

But to be honest he wasn't the only pastor in town that wanted it. A church down the street asked to borrow it and two guys showed up, pulled it out of our crawl space, and hauled it to their truck.

You do have to wonder what the neighbors think about us.

And it does make shopping for Dave a little difficult. It's hard to know exactly what he will like.

I'm hoping he doesn't buy ME an urn.

Death, it really is an awful thing. It's scary funny to think about caskets under the house. It's almost never, unless you're Dave, that people buy them just to wait for the right moment to use them. The truth is death frightens us. We do not want to think about death, to even consider our own mortality. But death comes. Satan said it wouldn't. But God said it would, and it did, and it does, and it will continue to be so for each and every one of us.

Death seems like a bleak way to end a book on new beginnings, but we can because death is NOT the final word.

Genesis 3, Matthew 28

Now death lived in the world.

Death had reached out its hand and Adam and Eve had grabbed hold. But it wasn't just death for them. It was death for everything. Every living thing now had a death sentence pronounced over it.

But that is not the end of the story.

Thousands of years later, Jesus Christ, the Messiah, the Savior of the world had a death sentence pronounced over Him. He took His last breath. He was dead.

The sadness and grief were overwhelming. The women went to the tomb. Jesus was dead and His body needed preparation.

They went expecting to deal with death, but instead they met life.

"The angel said to the women, 'Do not be afraid, for I know that you are looking for Jesus, who was crucified. He is not here; He has risen, just as He said. Come and see the place where He lay. Then go quickly and tell His disciples: He has risen from the dead and is going ahead of you into Galilee. There you will see Him. Now I have told you.'"
Matthew 28:5-7

You see Jesus Christ arose. Death could not hold Him because Jesus conquered all sin.

Death had come into the world because of one sin. Jesus died for all sins.

The best news in all the world is that Jesus Christ rose from the dead. On that beautiful, glorious morning, the world had a Savior. Every sin was covered, every sinner included. Death could not keep Jesus in the grave because sin was no match for Him.

Please understand this, every sin you have ever committed was covered on that day. Every evil, unkind thought, every wicked deed was paid for and because of that you can walk in freedom. You don't have to be held in sin's grasp.

His life was bigger than sin and death and He offers His triumphant eternal life to you.

A new beginning? Oh my yes.

It's a new start, a new life, a new direction, a new eternity.

But it is, after all, just a beginning. You see one of these days our breath will catch in our throats and we will look into the most beautiful eyes we have ever seen. We will hear His voice that echoes through the universe. He will lift us in His arms and carry us over the threshold into that blissful place called Heaven.

Take a deep breath...we're home.

Learn More

Learn more, explore additional writings,
and contact K.L. Kandel at **www.klkandel.com**.